Vegetarian
COOKING

SUSIE WARD

A QUINTET BOOK

ISBN: 0-7858-0494-3

This book was designed and produced by
Quintet Publishing Limited

Designer: Melanie Williams
Project Editors: Laura Sandelson, Damien Thompson
Editor: Susie Ward
Jacket Design: Nik Morley

Typeset in Great Britain by
Central Southern Typesetters, Eastbourne

Produced in Australia by Griffin Colour

Published by Chartwell Books
A Division of Book Sales, Inc.
P.O. Box 7100
Edison, New Jersey 08818-7100

CONTENTS

INTRODUCTION

Vegetarian food is different, delicious, nourishing and fresh. It can turn cooking, as well as eating, into a daily pleasure. The simple goodness of fresh ingredients in a loaf of home-made bread and a bowl of soup often give more satisfaction than the most complicated concoction smothered in butter-rich sauce. Learning to cook without meat and even most fish is something of a challenge, so used are we all to having one or the other as the main dish of the meal.

Vegetarianism and wholefood cookery are enjoying a new surge of popularity in the developed world as a reaction to the high-fat, high-sugar, high-starch junk foods that have so dominated our diets for the past 30 years.

The first pleasure of wholefood cookery is the goodness it brings to your table. The freshness and flavour of natural foods, unrefined and free from additives, offers a range of ingredients that is infinitely rich and subtle. But wholefood eating doesn't only satisfy the palate, it brings long-term health benefits too.

Our Western diet tends to be soft, sweet and high in animal fats. Over-refined and processed foods contain fewer vitamins and minerals, and chemical additives can cause unpleasant side effects. The foods closest to nature - fresh fruit and vegetables, unrefined grains, nuts and pulses - are high in vitamins and minerals, high in fibre and low in fat. They provide cheaper protein and satisfy at moderate calorie levels.

So vegetarianism also makes economic and ecological sense. A field of soya beans will yield 30 times as much protein as the same field given over to the rearing of beef cattle. Surprisingly though, it is still the case that agricultural land is devoted to feeding animals, far more than to growing crops. A further cruel reality is that economic pressures tend to encourage under-developed countries to export their grain as cattle feed for richer countries.

For many people, it is the slaughter of animals for food which has made them turn to a vegetarian life, as has the practice of keeping battery hens in tiny cages for the duration of their short lives. In addition, though modern food production methods have effectively made meat much cheaper than ever before, inevitably the taste of mass-produced meat, from animals reared on chemically treated feed and injected with hormones, suffers from a uniform blandness. A true free

range chicken is practically impossible to buy in the Western world – in America 98 per cent of chickens are battery reared. Considerations such as this have given many a less ideological but as valid a reason to prefer a largely wholefood and vegetarian lifestyle.

Other healthy products - for instance yoghurt, complement much vegetarian fare. It is perhaps the best known of all cultured milk products and has had an amazing rise from relative obscurity as an indigenous Middle Eastern food to a world-wide popularity - all within the last 20 or so years. It has been credited with extraordinary properties, particularly since scientists about 100 years ago became fascinated by the microbiological processes which take place in milk during fermentation. At that time a Russian scientist, Ilya Mechnikov, isolated the bacteria found in yoghurt. It is recorded that ancient physicians used to prescribe sour milk for dysentery, tuberculosis, liver problems and various other illnesses. It was found that an acid milk is more easily digested than ordinary milk, and modern medical practitioners have used it to counteract the effect of some antibiotics which destroy beneficial intestinal flora. Today aficionados of yoghurt are able to enjoy a wide selection of the product and the truly devoted sleuth may be able to track down some very unusual varieties.

So you see, you don't have to be vegetarian to enjoy this book, but you might adopt a new attitude to eating. For instance, you could break away from the traditional three-course meal and serve several complementary dishes at once, as in Eastern countries, or you could serve one large salad as a main course and offer home-made bread and an assortment of dressings. The best thing about vegetarianism is that it is an adventure and opens new possibilities to the diner, and to the cook.

Harvest Soup

INGREDIENTS *serves 4-6*

1-2 tsp/5-10ml oil
1 onion, chopped
2¼ cups/350g/12oz pumpkin, peeled
  and diced
2 cups/250g/8oz carrots, sliced
2 potatoes
juice of half a lemon
5 cups/1.1l/2pts stock
salt and freshly ground black pepper
1 courgette, sliced (optional)
⅓ cup/50g/2oz runner beans, sliced
  (optional)
basil leaves to garnish

METHOD

Heat oil in a large saucepan and fry onion until translucent.

Add pumpkin, carrots and potatoes and pour over lemon juice. Sweat, covered, for 5 minutes.

Add stock and seasoning and simmer until potatoes are cooked. Blend or part-blend the soup.

If liked, add courgettes and beans and simmer for a further 4 minutes. Check seasoning.

Serve garnished with basil leaves. This soup can also be served sprinkled with Parmesan cheese.

▼ Harvest soup

Cream of Cauliflower Soup

INGREDIENTS *serves 4*
1 small cauliflower
salt and freshly ground black pepper
4 tbsp/50g/2oz butter
¼ cup/25g/1oz plain untreated flour
6 tbsp/120ml/4fl oz single cream
1-2 egg yolks
1 tbsp/15ml chopped chives

METHOD
Trim the outer leaves off the cauliflower and steam it whole in boiling salted water in a pan with the lid on until tender. Allow the cauliflower to cool and reserve the water.

Melt the butter in a saucepan and stir in the flour. Gradually stir in the cauliflower water, made up to 3¾ cups/900ml/1½pts with fresh water.

Reserve some of the cauliflower florets for garnishing. Discard the tougher stalks and purée the rest in a blender. Add to the saucepan.

Beat the cream and egg yolks together in a bowl. Beat in some of the soup, then return to the pan. Add reserved cauliflower florets. Heat through but do not boil. Season and add chopped chives. Serve with triangles of hot toast.

Garlic Soup

INGREDIENTS *serves 4-6*
5 cups/1.1l/2pts vegetable stock
4 garlic cloves, crushed
3 level tsp/15ml paprika
3 level tsp/15ml cumin
salt and pepper
2 pieces bread, toasted
oil
6 eggs (optional)

METHOD
Pour vegetable stock into a pan, add the garlic, paprika and cumin, and bring to the boil. Season.

Break the toast into cubes and put into hot soup bowls.

Place a pan on the heat, lightly oil and fry the eggs until the white forms. Tip out 1 egg into each soup bowl and pour over the boiling soup.

Cheese and Onion Soup

INGREDIENTS *serves 4-6*
1-2 tbsp/15-30ml oil
2 medium onions, sliced
5 cups/1.1l/2pts stock
250g/8oz potatoes
1½ cups/175g/6oz grated
   cheddar cheese
salt
soy sauce

METHOD
Heat oil in a large saucepan and stir-fry onions until lightly browned. Add stock and bring to the boil.

Meanwhile, peel the potatoes and grate them into the saucepan. Turn down the heat and simmer until potatoes have cooked and soup has thickened.

Add the grated cheese, stirring to melt. Season to taste with salt and soy sauce. Serve with wholewheat bread and a crisp green salad.

Butterbean and Mushroom Chowder

INGREDIENTS *serves 4-6*
1 cup/100g/4oz butter beans soaked
   overnight in cold water
1 tsp/5ml olive oil
2 onions, chopped
2 stalks celery, sliced
8oz/225g potatoes, peeled and diced
4oz/100g button mushrooms, sliced
½ cup/50g/2oz sweetcorn kernels
1¼ cups/300ml/½pt skimmed milk
salt and freshly ground black pepper
2 tbsp/30ml chopped parsley

METHOD
Drain the beans and place in a large saucepan covered with fresh water. Boil fast for 10 minutes, then simmer for a further 35-40 minutes, or until soft.

Drain the beans and reserve 2 cups/450ml/¾pt of the stock.

Heat the oil in a large saucepan and gently fry the onion. Add the celery and potato and cook for 2-3 minutes, stirring from time to time. Add the reserved stock and mushrooms, bring to the boil, cover and simmer for 10 minutes.

Red-Hot Lentil Soup

INGREDIENTS *serves 6*
3 tbsp/40g/1½oz butter
1 large onion, chopped
1 clove garlic, chopped
1 slice fresh ginger root, unpeeled
1 slice lemon
1⅛ cups/225g/8oz red lentils
7 cups/1.5l/2¾pts water
salt
pinch of paprika
1 green chilli, deseeded and chopped

METHOD
Heat 2 tbsp/25g/1oz butter in a pan and add the onion, garlic, ginger and lemon. Sweat with the lid on over a low heat for 5 minutes.

Add the lentils and the water (small red lentils do not need to be presoaked) and season with salt and paprika. Cook for about 40 minutes until lentils have thickened the soup.

Heat the remaining butter in a pan and quickly fry the chilli. Serve the soup with chilli topping.

Mushroom Soup

INGREDIENTS *serves 6*
butter or oil
1 large onion, sliced
6 cups/350g/12oz sliced mushrooms
grated nutmeg
1 tbsp/15ml flour
2 cups/450ml/¾pt vegetable stock
1¼ cups/300ml/½pt yoghurt
2 tbsp/30ml sherry (optional)

METHOD
Heat the butter and cook the onion until it has just softened but not browned. Add the mushrooms, stir and leave them to cook for 2 minutes. Add more butter if necessary.

Add the nutmeg and flour and stir well. Slowly add the stock, stirring until the mixture is smooth.

Bring the soup to the boil sand then simmer for 5 minutes. Stir in the yoghurt and just warm it through. Add the sherry. Serve hot.

Cream of Nettle Soup

INGREDIENTS *serves 6*
2lb/900g young nettles
2 tbsp/25g/1oz butter
1 small onion, chopped
¼ cup/25g/1oz flour
3¾ cups/900ml/30fl oz milk
salt and freshly ground black pepper
2 egg yolks
1 tbsp/15ml single cream
cream and croûtons to serve

METHOD
Pick the young nettle leaves before the plants flower. Discard the stalks, wash the leaves and press them into a pan with only the water that is clinging to them. Cover the pan and cook until soft (5-8 minutes). Purée in a blender.

Heat the butter in a pan and cook the onion until soft. Stir in the flour. Stir in a little milk and cook until thick. Stir in enough of the remaining milk to make a very thin sauce. Add the milk and the sauce to the nettles. Season well.

Beat the egg yolks with the cream. Stir in a little of the soup, then return to the pan. Heat through and check seasoning.

To serve, add a swirl of cream and some croûtons to each individual bowl.

▲ ▲ Red-hot lentil soup
▲ Cream of nettle soup

Carrot and Coriander Soup

INGREDIENTS *serves 6-8*
oil or butter
1 medium onion, sliced
9 cups/700g/1½lbs carrots, sliced
1 tsp/5ml ground coriander
3¾ cups/900ml/1½pts vegetable stock
⅔ cup/150ml/¼pt soured cream
salt and freshly ground black pepper
parsley to garnish

METHOD

Heat the oil, add the onion and cook until it has just softened but not browned. Add the carrots and coriander and stir well. Leave the carrots to cook gently for 3 minutes.

Pour in the stock and bring the mixture to the boil, then simmer, covered, for 25 minutes.

Liquidize the soup, adding the soured cream. Adjust the seasoning. Serve very cold, garnished with parsley.

Gazpacho

INGREDIENTS *serves 4-6*
1lb/450g large ripe tomatoes
1 large onion
2 cloves garlic
1 green pepper
1 red pepper
½ cucumber
2 slices wholewheat bread
3 tbsp/45ml olive oil
3 tbsp/45ml wine vinegar
1¼ cups/300ml/½pt tomato juice
1¼ cups/300ml/½pt water
salt and freshly ground black pepper

METHOD

Skin tomatoes, discard seeds and juice and chop the flesh. Peel and finely chop the onion and garlic. Remove pith and seeds from peppers and dice. Peel and dice the cucumber. Cut the crusts from the bread and dice.

Put vegetables and bread in a large bowl, pour over the remaining ingredients, stir and season. Chill well - overnight is best for a good tasty soup.

You can partly blend the soup if you wish, or blend all of it, in which case offer small bowls of chopped onions, tomatoes, peppers, cucumber and croûtons as a garnish.

Broccoli and Orange Soup

INGREDIENTS *serves 6*
1 medium onion, chopped
1 tbsp/15ml oil
1lb/450g broccoli, chopped
juice of 2 oranges
2½ cups/600ml/1pt vegetable stock
1¼ cups/300ml/½pt yoghurt
1 tbsp/15ml cornstarch
2 tbsp/30ml water
salt and freshly ground black pepper

METHOD

(Reserve some small pieces of broccoli for garnish, together with a little grated orange rind.) Heat the oil and cook the onion until it has just softened but not browned. Add the broccoli and stir round. Cook, covered, for a few minutes and then add the orange juice and stock. Bring to the boil, cover and simmer for about 20 minutes, until the broccoli is soft. Purée the soup in a blender. Mix the cornstarch and water to a smooth paste and stir into the soup with salt and pepper to taste. Return the soup to the heat and cook for a further five minutes. Serve, garnished with the reserved broccoli and the orange rind.

Use frozen broccoli if fresh is not available. Serve cold if preferred.

Hummus

INGREDIENTS *serves 4*
1¼ cups/225g/8oz dried chick peas,
   soaked overnight
1 bouquet garni
1 small onion, sliced
2 cloves garlic, crushed
juice of 2 lemons
4 tbsp/60ml/2oz tahini paste
3 tbsp/45ml olive oil
salt and freshly ground black pepper
1 tomato, sliced
sprig of parsley

METHOD
Drain the chick peas and place in a large
saucepan with plenty of water, the bouquet
garni and onion. Bring to the boil then
simmer gently for 1¼-2 hours, or until
tender.

Drain, reserving a little of the cooking
liquid. Discard the onion and bouquet
garni.

Place the garlic, lemon juice, tahini, olive
oil and seasoning in a food processor or
blender. Add the cooked chick peas and
process to a smooth paste.

Add a little of the reserved cooking liquid
if the paste is too thick, and stir rapidly.

Arrange the hummus in a dish, edge with
halved tomato slices and garnish with
parsley. Serve with warmed pitta bread.

Guacamole

INGREDIENTS *serves 2-4*
2 large ripe avocados
2 large ripe tomatoes
1 bunch spring onions
1-2 tbsp/15-30ml olive oil
1-2 tbsp/15-30ml lemon juice
salt and freshly ground black pepper
2 green chillies

METHOD
Remove the flesh from the avocados and
mash. Skin the tomatoes, remove the seeds
and chop finely. Chop the spring onions.

Mix vegetables together with olive oil
and lemon juice and season to taste.
Garnish with chopped green chillies and
serve, chilled, as a dip or with hot pitta
bread (see page 151).

Stuffed Tomatoes

INGREDIENTS *serves 4*
8 English (small) tomatoes, or 3 beef
 (large) tomatoes
4 hard-boiled eggs, cooled and peeled
6 tbsp/90ml mayonnaise
1 tsp/5ml garlic paste
salt and freshly ground black pepper
1 tbsp/15ml parsley, chopped
1 tbsp/15ml white breadcrumbs for the
 beef (large) tomatoes

METHOD
Skin the tomatoes, first by cutting out the
core with a sharp knife and making a '+'
incision on the other end of the tomato.
Then place in a pan of boiling water for 10
seconds, remove and plunge into a bowl of
iced or very cold water (this latter step is to
stop the tomatoes from cooking and going
mushy).

Slice the tops off the tomatoes, and just
enough of their bases to remove the rounded
ends so that the tomatoes will sit squarely
on the plate. Keep the tops if using small
tomatoes, but not for the large tomatoes.

Remove the seeds and inside, either with
a teaspoon or small, sharp knife. Mash the
eggs with the mayonnaise, garlic paste, salt,
pepper and parsley.

Fill the tomatoes, firmly pressing the
filling down. With small tomatoes, replace
the lids at a jaunty angle. If keeping to serve
later, brush them with olive oil and black
pepper to prevent from drying out. Cover
with plastic film and keep.

NOTE
For large tomatoes, the filling must be very
firm, so it can be sliced. If you make your
own mayonnaise, thicken it by using more
egg yolks. If you use shop-bought mayonnaise, add enough white breadcrumbs until
the mixture is the consistency of mashed
potatoes. Season well, to taste. Fill the
tomatoes, pressing down firmly until level.
Refrigerate for 1 hour, then slice with a
sharp carving knife into rings. Sprinkle with
chopped parsley.

▲ ◀ Stuffed tomatoes

◀ Babagannouch

Babagannouch

INGREDIENTS *serves 6-8*
3 aubergines
4 cloves garlic
2 tbsp/30ml tahini
½ tsp/2½g cumin seeds
½ tsp/2½g chilli powder
juice of 3 lemons
salt to taste
chopped parsley
olives

METHOD
Grill aubergines until the skin blackens.
Cool slightly in a paper bag and peel off
most of the charred skin.

Mash the softened aubergine with the
remaining ingredients and blend until fully
combined. Garnish with parsley and olives
and serve warm with pitta bread.

Courgette Moulds

INGREDIENTS *serves 4*
1lb/450g courgettes, sliced
1 onion, chopped
2 tbsp/30ml lemon juice
2 tsp/10ml fresh coriander leaves, chopped
4oz/100g fromage blanc
salt and freshly ground black pepper
1 sachet agar-agar
2/3 cup/150ml/1/4pt natural low fat yoghurt
5 tbsp/75ml/3fl oz skimmed milk
1 egg yolk
1 tsp/5ml curry paste

METHOD
Place the courgettes and onions in a saucepan with 2×15ml sp/2 tbsp water and the lemon juice. Cover and cook over a gentle heat for 8-10 minutes, or until softened.

Cool slightly and purée in a food processor or blender. Add the coriander leaves, cheese and seasoning and purée until smooth. Leave until lukewarm.

Sprinkle the agar-agar over 2 tbsp/30ml water in a cup. Stand in a saucepan of hot water and stir to dissolve. Add to the purée and pour into four 2/3 cup/150ml/1/4pt ramekin dishes. Chill for 1-1½ hours until set.

Meanwhile mix the yoghurt, milk, egg yolk and curry paste together and heat gently until slightly thickened. Do not boil. Leave to cool.

Pour the sauce across the base of a serving dish, loosen the moulds and turn out on to the dish. Garnish the tops of the moulds with chervil and serve.

Mozzarella and Avocado Bees

INGREDIENTS *serves 2*
1 ripe avocado
4oz/100g Mozzarella cheese
1 tbsp/15ml olive oil
1 tbsp/15ml tarragon vinegar
salt and freshly ground black pepper

METHOD
Cut the avocado in half and remove the stone. With a palette knife carefully remove the skin from each half of the avocado. Lay the avocado halves flat-side downwards and cut horizontally into 1/4in/1cm slices.

Cut semi-circular slices from the Mozzarella, with 4 extra semi-circles for wings.

Arrange the cheese slices between the avocado slices to form the striped body of the bee, and arrange the wings at the sides.

Mix the oil and vinegar together and season well. Pour over the bees and serve.

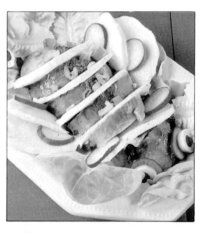

Vegetables in Agar-agar

INGREDIENTS *serves 4*
2½ cups/600ml/20fl oz dissolved agar-agar or other vegetable gelatine
1 cup/100g/4oz peeled and diced carrot
1 cup/100g/4oz trimmed and sliced green beans
1 tbsp/15ml walnut oil
1 cup/100g/4oz sliced button mushrooms
1 tbsp/15ml stuffed olives, sliced
2/3 cup/150ml/1/4 pt thick mayonnaise

METHOD
In water dissolve enough agar-agar or equivalent vegetable gelatine, following directions on the packet, to make 2½ cups/600ml/20fl oz. Allow it to cool. Chill a mould. Wet the mould and when the aspic is almost set, line the mould with it. Place in the fridge to set.

Meanwhile cook the carrot and green beans in salted water until tender. Refresh in cold water. Heat the walnut oil in a pan and gently sauté the mushrooms. Allow to cool.

Mix the vegetables together with the olives, mayonnaise and the remaining aspic and fill the mould. Chill until set.

Dip the mould into hot water and turn out onto a plate. Cut into wedges and serve each wedge with a crisp lettuce leaf and a triange of wholemeal toast.

◀ Mozzarella and avocado bees
▼ Courgette moulds

Devilled Eggs

INGREDIENTS *serves 4*
4 hard-boiled eggs, cut in half,
  lengthwise
1½ tbsp/23g onions, finely chopped
2 green chillis, finely chopped
1 tbsp/5ml coriander leaves, chopped
½ tsp/2.5ml salt
2 tbsp/30g mashed potatoes
oil for deep frying
1 tbsp/15ml plain flour
2fl oz/60ml/¼ cup water

METHOD

Remove the yolks and mix with the onions, chillis, coriander leaves, salt and mashed potatoes. Put the mixture back into the egg whites. Chill for 30 minutes.

Heat the oil in a karai over high heat. While the oil is heating up make a batter with the flour and water. Be careful not to allow the oil to catch fire.

Dip the eggs into the batter and slip into the hot oil. Fry until golden, turning once.

Stuffed Aubergines

INGREDIENTS *serves 4-8*
4 aubergines
olive oil
1 large onion, chopped
2-3 cloves garlic, crushed
4 large tomatoes, skinned and chopped
2 tbsp/10g fresh herbs, chopped
salt and freshly ground black pepper
4oz/100g Mozzarella cheese
4 tbsp/60ml brown breadcrumbs
a little butter

METHOD

Preheat the oven to 400°F/200°C/Gas 6. Wash the aubergines. Cut in half lengthwise and score the cut surface deeply with a knife. Sprinkle with salt and leave, cut surface down, for 30 minutes.

Meanwhile heat 1-2 tbsp/15-30ml oil in a pan and fry the onion and garlic until translucent. Transfer to a bowl and mix in the tomatoes and chopped herbs.

Add more oil to the pan. Rinse the aubergines and pat dry. Place them cut surface down in the pan and cook gently for about 15 minutes. They absorb a lot of oil,

▼ Stuffed aubergines   ▲ Devilled eggs

so you will need to keep adding a little more.

Scoop some of the flesh out of the aubergines, mash and mix it with the rest of the filling. Season well. Pile the filling onto the aubergines and top with thinly sliced Mozzarella. Sprinkle with breadcrumbs and dot with butter. Place aubergines in a greased ovenproof dish and bake for 20 minutes until the cheese has melted and the breadcrumbs are crispy.

13

Orange and Walnut Salad

INGREDIENTS *serves 4*
3 plump heads chicory
2 large sweet oranges, peel and pith
    removed, segmented
3oz/75g walnuts, chopped

MUSTARD DRESSING
2 tbsp/30ml walnut oil
pinch mustard powder
1 tbsp/15ml orange juice
1 tbsp/15ml lemon juice

METHOD
Mix the chicory slices, oranges and half the walnuts together and place in a serving dish.

Sprinkle over the remaining walnuts.

Whisk the walnut oil and mustard powder together, then gradually whisk in the orange and lemon juices.

Pour the dressing over the salad and serve immediately.

Mixed Greens and Mushrooms with Raspberry Vinaigrette

INGREDIENTS *serves 4*
4 tbsp/60g pine nuts
2 heads cabbage lettuce or other soft
lettuce
2 heads chicory
1 small head radicchio
8oz/225g stemmed small mushrooms

RASPBERRY VINAIGRETTE
4 tbsp/60ml olive oil
2 tbsp/30ml raspberry vinegar
1 finely chopped shallot
1 tsp/5ml Dijon-style mustard
2 tsp/10ml single cream
salt and freshly ground black pepper to
    taste

METHOD
Pre-heat the oven to 350°F/180°C/Gas 4. Place the pine nuts in a shallow baking dish and toast them in the oven until lightly browned, about 5 minutes. Remove from oven and set aside.

Wash and gently dry the cabbage lettuce, chicory and radicchio. Tear the lettuce and radicchio into bite-sized pieces. Cut the chicory into thin slices. Put the greens into a large salad bowl. Add the mushrooms and toasted pine nuts.

In a mixing bowl combine the olive oil, vinegar, shallot, mustard, cream, salt and pepper. Whisk until the vinaigrette is smooth and well blended.

Pour the vinaigrette over the greens and toss well. Serve at once.

▲ ◄ Orange and walnut salad
◄ Mixed greens and mushroom salad

Curly Endive and Alfalfa Salad

INGREDIENTS *serves 4-6*

¹/₂ small curly endive, torn into pieces

40oz/100g alfalfa sprouts

2oz/50g small button mushrooms, thinly sliced

¹/₂ red pepper, sliced

DRESSING

juice 1 lemon

2tsp/10ml olive oil

1 small onion, grated

¹/₄tsp/1.5g Chinese five spice powder

METHOD

Arrange the curly endive on a large serving plate or 4 individual plates.

Mix the alfalfa, mushrooms and pepper together in a bowl.

Mix the dressing ingredients together and add to the bowl of vegetables. Toss well and arrange on top of the lettuce.

California Waldorf Salad

INGREDIENTS *serves 6*

3¹/₂oz/90g mung bean sprouts or alfalfa sprouts

3 tart apples, cored and diced but not peeled

1lb/450g celery, chopped

¹/₂ cup/50g/2oz slivered almonds

3 large mushrooms, coarsely chopped

8fl oz/250ml Yoghurt Mayonnaise

10 lettuce leaves

3¹/₂oz/90g seedless grapes, halved

METHOD

Blanch the bean sprouts in a pan of boiling water for 45 seconds. Drain and rinse in cold water. Drain well again. Coarsely chop the bean sprouts.

Put the apple, celery, almonds and mushrooms in a large mixing bowl. Mix well with a wooden spoon.

Add the Yoghurt Mayonnaise and mix thoroughly.

Line a serving platter with the lettuce leaves. Mound the bean sprouts in the centre. Transfer the mixed ingredients to the platter and garnish with the halved grapes.

Classic Waldorf Salad

INGREDIENTS *serves 2 - 4*

8 stalks crisp celery

2 rosy-skinned dessert apples

lemon juice

¹/₂ cup/50g/2oz walnuts

6 tbsp/90ml good mayonnaise

salt and freshly ground black pepper

METHOD

If the celery is not crisp, immerse it in ice-cold water. It will soon freshen up. Pat dry and slice.

Core the apples but do not peel - the pink skin will give colour contrast to the salad. Slice and sprinkle with lemon juice to prevent discolouring. Toss all the ingredients in the mayonnaise and season well.

VARIATION

This salad also tastes good with blue cheese dressing. Blend the mayonnaise with 1 tbsp blue cheese before adding to the salad.

▲ ▲ Curly endive and alfalfa salad

▲ California Waldorf salad

Lentil and Feta Cheese Salad

INGREDIENTS *serves 6*
2 cups/350g/12oz brown lentils
1 bay leaf
$\frac{1}{2}$ tsp/2.5ml dried basil
2 garlic cloves, crushed
stalk celery, finely chopped
1 small onion, chopped
3 tbsp/45ml fresh chives, chopped
1$\frac{1}{2}$ cups/175g/6oz crumbled feta cheese
6 tbsp/90ml/3fl oz virgin olive oil
3 tbsp/45ml wine vinegar
$\frac{1}{8}$ tsp/large pinch dried oregano
salt and freshly ground black pepper

METHOD
Put the lentils in a bowl. Add 3 cups/750ml/
1$\frac{1}{4}$pts cold water and soak the lentils for 2 hours. Drain.

Put the lentils in a saucepan and add enough cold water to cover them completely. Add the bay leaf, basil and 1 garlic clove. Bring to the boil and simmer, covered, for 20 minutes.

Add the celery and onion. Add enough additional water to cover the lentils. Cover the saucepan and simmer for 10 more minutes.

Drain the lentils, celery and onion and discard the bay leaf and garlic clove. Put the lentils, celery and onion in a serving bowl. Add the chives and feta cheese. Toss.

Put the olive oil, vinegar, oregano, remaining garlic clove, salt and pepper in a jar with a tightly fitting lid. Cover tightly and shake until well blended.

Pour the dressing over the lentil salad and toss. Let the salad stand for 2 hours, tossing occasionally, before serving.

Egg and Pasta Salad

INGREDIENTS *serves 4*
1 cup/225g/8oz green or wholewheat
  pasta shapes
2 tsp/10ml oil
4 eggs
1 cup/100g/4oz green beans
2 stalks celery
1 dessert apple
$\frac{1}{2}$ cup/50g/2oz walnuts
Mayonnaise
salt and freshly ground black pepper
1-2 tbsp/15-30ml dill

METHOD
Cook the pasta in plenty of boiling salted water, to which you have added oil, until al dente. Drain and allow to cool.

Hard boil the eggs, peel under cold running water and allow to cool. Cut into quarters.

Top and tail the beans and cut into manageable lengths. Simmer in salted water until cooked but not soft. Drain and allow to cool.

Chop the celery. Peel, core and dice the apple. Toss all the ingredients except the eggs together in the Mayonnaise. Season and garnish with eggs and dill.

Haricot Bean Salad

INGREDIENTS *serves 4*
1 cup/175g/6oz dried haricot beans,
  soaked overnight
2 cloves garlic, crushed
2 tbsp/30ml wine vinegar
2 tbsp/30ml olive oil
1 tsp/5ml French mustard
salt and freshly ground black pepper
1 red pepper, seeded and thinly sliced
1 leek, thinly sliced
2 spring onions, green and white parts
  chopped separately

METHOD
Place the beans in a large saucepan and coker with fresh water. Bring to the boil and boil fast for 10 minutes, then cover and simmer for 40-50 minutes or until tender. Drain.

Combine the garlic, vinegar, olive oil, mustard and seasoning in a screw top jar, seal and shake well.

Pour over the hot beans and leave to cool. Stir in the pepper, leek and white parts of the spring onions and place in a serving dish.

Sprinkle with green chopped onions and serve.

▲ Haricot bean salad

Asparagus Pancakes

INGREDIENTS *serves 2*
1 small clove garlic, crushed
2 tbsp/15g/¹/₂oz chopped fresh basil
  leaves
1 tbsp/25g/1oz pine kernels
3 tbsp/45ml Parmesan cheese, grated
2 tbsp/30ml olive oil
salt and freshly ground black pepper
6 tbsp/40g/1¹/₂oz plain wholewheat
  flour
2 tbsp/15g/¹/₂oz buckwheat flour
1 egg, lightly beaten
²/₃ cup/150ml/¹/₄pt skimmed milk
200g/7oz frozen asparagus spears
3 tomatoes, skinned, seeded and
  chopped

METHOD
Place the garlic, basil, pine kernels and 2 tbsp/30ml Parmesan cheese in a food processor or blender and purée. With the motor running gradually add the oil and blend to a smooth sauce. Season to taste.

Place the flours in a bowl, gradually add the egg and milk, beating well to form a smooth batter.

Heat a lightly oiled 18cm/7in heavy based frying pan. Pour in sufficient batter to thinly coat the base.

Cook for 1-2 minutes, loosen the edge, turn or toss and cook the second side. Transfer to a plate and keep hot. Repeat with the remaining batter to make 4 pancakes. Stack the pancakes with greaseproof paper between them and keep warm.

Place the asparagus in a saucepan, pour over just sufficient boiling water to cover and simmer for 6 minutes.

Divide the asparagus between the pancakes, top with sauce and fold up. Place in a shallow ovenproof dish, sprinkle with tomatoes and remaining cheese.

Place under a grill until browned.

Pancakes

INGREDIENTS *Makes 5 cups/1.1l/2 pints*
2¹/₂ cups/600ml/1pt milk
2¹/₄ cups/225g/8oz flour
pinch salt
2 eggs
butter or oil for frying

METHOD
Mix the milk and flour together until smooth. Add the salt and eggs and beat in well.

Heat a little butter or oil in a heavy pan (preferably one used only for pancakes). Tip out excess butter.

Pour in just enough batter to coat the bottom of the pan. Fry on one side only if the pancakes are to be filled.

Mushroom Pancakes

INGREDIENTS *serves 4*
1 recipe pancakes
2 tbsp/25g/1oz butter
1 large onion, finely chopped
4 cups/450g/1lb mushrooms, chopped
2 tbsp/25g/1oz canned red pimentos,
  finely chopped
²/₃ cup/150ml/¹/₄pt soured cream
salt and freshly ground black pepper
melted butter

METHOD
Make the pancakes and keep warm.

Melt the butter, and the onion and cook until it has softened but not browned. Add the mushrooms and cook until soft. Drain off excess liquid. Mix in the pimentos, soured cream, salt and pepper.

Put a spoonful of the mixture on to each pancake on the cooked side. Roll up the pancakes, tucking in the edges.

Place the rolled pancakes in a buttered oven dish, drizzle a little melted butter over the top. Warm through in the oven at 350°F/180°C/Gas 4 for 25 minutes.

Serve with more soured cream if desired.

▲ Asparagus pancakes

Stuffed Cheese Pancakes

INGREDIENTS *serves 3-4*
³⁄₈ cup/40g/1¹⁄₂oz plain untreated flour
³⁄₈ cup/40g/1¹⁄₂oz wholewheat flour
pinch salt
1 egg
²⁄₃ cup/150ml/5fl oz milk
1 tbsp/15ml melted butter

CHEESE AND HERB FILLING
2 cups/450g/1lb curd or cottage cheese
2 tbsp/30ml cream
1 fat clove garlic, crushed
2 tbsp/30ml finely chopped fresh herbs
1 tbsp/15ml chopped spring onion

METHOD
To make the pancake batter, sift the flour and salt into a bowl. Make a well in the middle of it and add the egg. Gradually beat in the milk. When half of the milk has been added, beat in the melted butter. Continue beating in the milk until you have a thin batter. Allow the batter to stand for half an hour.

Meanwhile, prepare the filling. Combine the curd cheese with the rest of the ingredients and mix well.

To make the pancakes, oil a heavy-bottomed frying pan 7in/18cm in diameter. Place it on the flame and when it is very hot, add 2 tbsp/30ml of the batter. Tilt the pan so that the batter covers the base. Cook until the pancake is beginning to brown on the underside and then turn over and cook the top. You may have to throw the first pancake away, as it will absorb the excess oil in the pan.

Continue making pancakes, keeping them warm, until all the batter is used up. Divide the filling between them, rolling the pancakes around it into a cigar shape. Arrange the stuffed pancakes in an ovenproof dish and heat in a moderate oven for about 1¹⁄₂ minutes.

Genoese Pasta with Pesto Sauce

INGREDIENTS *serves 4-6*
2 tbsp/25g/1oz fresh basil leaves
2 cloves garlic
pinch salt
¹⁄₂ cup/50g/2oz pine kernels
¹⁄₂ cup/50g/2oz Parmesan cheese
¹⁄₂ cup/100ml/4fl oz olive oil
1lb/450g spaghetti or tagliatelle, cooked and drained
2 tbsp/25g/1oz butter

METHOD
Blend the basil leaves in a liquidizer. Add the crushed cloves of garlic and olive oil. Process for a few seconds.

Gradually add the pine kernels, Parmesan cheese, season remembering that Parmesan has a salty taste. The consistency should be thick and creamy.

Melt the butter in the saucepan and reheat the cooked pasta. Remove from the heat and mix 2 tbsp/25g/1oz pesto with the pasta. Serve on individual plates with a spoonful of pesto on each helping. Parmesan can be added last.

NOTE
The pesto is never heated. It can be served at the table but make sure the pasta is hot.

Fettucini Romana

INGREDIENTS *serves 4*
1lb/450g fettucini
4 tbsp/50g/2oz butter
¹⁄₂ tsp/2.5ml ground nutmeg
²⁄₃ cup/150ml/¹⁄₄pt cream
salt and freshly ground black pepper
1 cup/100g/4oz Parmesan cheese

METHOD
Bring a well filled saucepan of salted water to the boil, add a few drops of oil and salt. Feed in the fettucini and cook until al dente - fresh pasta will only take about 2 minutes. Drain in a colander.

Melt the butter in the saucepan, add ground nutmeg. Pour in half the cream and stir until shiny and bubbles start to appear.

Add the fettucini and stir around in the pan. Pour in the remaining cream and cheese alternately, forking the pasta as it is mixed. Serve immediately.

NOTE
This is a real pasta-lovers' dish. To obtain best results use freshly grated Parmesan cheese rather than the commercially grated variety.

◀ Stuffed cheese pancakes
▶ Genoese pasta with pesto sauce

Tagliatelle with Sweet Pepper Sauce

INGREDIENTS *serves 4*
12oz/350g spinach tagliatelle noodles
2 tsp/10ml oil
$^{1}/_{2}$ tsp/2.5ml salt

THE SAUCE
1 small firm red pepper
1 small green pepper
1 small yellow pepper
1-2 tbsp/15-30ml olive oil
1 onion, chopped
2 cloves garlic, chopped
$1^{1}/_{2}$ cups/400g/15oz can tomatoes
1 tbsp/15ml tomato purée
fresh basil leaves, snipped
salt and freshly ground black pepper

METHOD
Trim and de-seed the peppers and cut into narrow strips. You can make the sauce with green peppers alone if you wish, but the red and yellow varieties are sweeter and make the dish look more colourful. Blanch the peppers for a minute in boiling salted water, refresh in cold water, then drain.

Heat the olive oil in a pan, add the garlic and onions and cook gently, stirring, until soft. Add the tomatoes, tomato purée and basil. Break up the tomatoes with a wooden spoon and simmer for about 5 minutes. Season to taste and blend the sauce in a blender. Return to the pan over a very low heat and add the peppers.

Cook the pasta in a large pan with plenty of water to which you have added a little oil and the salt. The water should be at a full rolling boil. The pasta will be ready in about 9 minutes. Drain and divide between individual warmed serving bowls.

Spoon the sauce over each helping of pasta and serve at once with Parmesan cheese.

▲ Spaghetti with Mascarpone
◀ Tagliatelle with sweet pepper sauce

Vegetarian Spaghetti Putanesca

INGREDIENTS *serves 4-6*
1 onion, peeled and diced
2 tbsp/30ml oil
2 cloves garlic, crushed
1 carrot, scraped and chopped
$1^{1}/_{2}$ cups/425g/15oz canned tomatoes
2 tomatoes, skinned and chopped
4 tbsp/60ml white wine
1 bay leaf
3-4 basil leaves or 1 tsp/15ml dried basil
salt and freshly ground pepper
1 tbsp/15ml capers, chopped
$^{1}/_{2}$ cup/50g/2oz stoned black olives
3 drops Tabasco sauce
1 tbsp/15ml freshly chopped parsley
450g/1lb cooked spaghetti
grated Parmesan cheese to serve

METHOD
Put the onion into the oil in a frying saucepan over a low heat. Allow to cook gently for 4 minutes, add the crushed garlic and carrots. Turn in the oil twice more.

Add the tomatoes, the white wine, bay leaf, basil and some seasoning. Bring to the boil and simmer for 30 minutes. Sieve or liquidize and return the sauce to the saucepan. Add the chopped capers, chopped olives and the spicy Tabasco sauce. Re-heat and serve over the pasta, with Parmesan cheese.

Spaghetti with Mascarpone

INGREDIENTS *serves 4*
12oz/350g wholewheat spaghetti
a little oil
100g/4oz Mascarpone or cream cheese
2 egg yolks
salt and freshly ground black pepper
grated Parmesan cheese to serve

METHOD
Cook the pasta in boiling salted water, to which you have added a few drops of oil, until *al dente.*

While you are draining the spaghetti, stir the egg yolks and Mascarpone together in a large pan over a low heat.

When the sauce begins to set, toss in the spaghetti. Serve at once with plenty of black pepper and Parmesan. This dish should be accompanied by a crunchy salad.

Pasta with Mushroom Sauce

INGREDIENTS *serves 1-2*
2-4 handfuls green pasta spirals
1 tsp/15ml oil
1 cup/50g/2oz mushrooms
milk
salt and freshly ground black pepper
yolk of 1 egg
1 tbsp/15ml cream
as much parsley as you like, chopped
Parmesan cheese, grated

METHOD
Cook the pasta in plenty of boiling salted water with 1 tsp/5ml oil, until al dente.

Meanwhile, wipe and slice the mushrooms. Place in a pan with a little milk, season well and poach gently, stirring, until soft and very black and the liquid has almost gone.

Beat the egg yolk with the cream and stir in the mushrooms.

Drain the pasta and stir in the mushroom mixture with plenty of parsley. Serve at once with Parmesan and a tender lettuce salad.

Spaghetti with Fresh Tomato and Basil Sauce

INGREDIENTS *serves 4*
2 tsp/10ml olive oil
1 onion, chopped
4 stalks celery, chopped
1 green chilli, seeded and finely chopped
2 cloves garlic, crushed
2¼ cups/700g/1½lb skinned and roughly
  chopped tomatoes
3 tbsp/45ml tomato purée
1 tbsp/15ml basil leaves, chopped
1 tbsp/15ml marjoram, chopped
12oz/350g wholewheat spaghetti or
  6oz/175g wholewheat spaghetti and
  6oz/175g spaghetti verdi
⅔ cup/50g/2oz black olives, stoned
3 tbsp/25g/1oz Parmesan cheese,
  grated
3 tbsp/25g/1oz pine kernels
basil sprigs

METHOD
Heat the oil in a saucepan, add the onion, celery, chilli and garlic and fry until soft. Add the tomatoes and tomato purée, 4 tbsp/60ml water, half the basil and marjoram. Bring to the boil and simmer for 10 minutes.

Place the wholewheat spaghetti in a large saucepan of boiling lightly salted water and cook for 12 minutes, or until just tender. Add the spaghetti verdi, if using, 2 minutes after the wholewheat spaghetti.

Drain the pasta and divide between 4 individual warmed plates. Stir the olives and remaining basil into the sauce and place on top of the spaghetti.

Sprinkle with cheese and nuts, garnish with basil sprigs and serve.

Vegetarian Bolonese Sauce

INGREDIENTS *serves 4-6*
1¼ cups/225g/8oz brown lentils
salt and freshly ground black pepper
1 bay leaf
1-2 tbsp/15-30ml olive oil
2 cloves garlic, chopped
1 onion, chopped
1 carrot, chopped
1 stick celery, chopped
1½ cups/400g/15oz can tomatoes,
  mashed
1 tbsp/15ml tomato purée
½ tsp/2.5ml dried mixed herbs
2 tbsp/30ml red wine
350g/12oz wholewheat or spinach pasta

METHOD
Soak the lentils overnight and simmer in salted water with a bay leaf until they can be mashed with a fork. Drain and discard the bayleaf.

Heat the oil in a pan and fry the onions and garlic until translucent. Add the carrot and celery and cook for a further 2 minutes.

Add the tomatoes and a little juice. Add the remaining ingredients and the lentils. Simmer until the sauce is quite thick. Blend or part-blend in a blender.

Serve the sauce in healthy spoonfuls over the warmed cooked pasta.

Hot Pasta Salad

INGREDIENTS *serves 4*
2 cloves garlic
3 tbsp/45ml olive oil
handful fresh basil leaves
1 tbsp/15ml grated Parmesan cheese

THE SALAD
4oz/100g Mozzarella cheese
1lb/450g Mediterranean tomatoes
1 cup/75g/3oz black olives
salt and freshly ground black pepper

THE PASTA
12oz/350g spinach pasta twists
1 tsp/5ml olive oil

METHOD
Chop the garlic and put it in a mortar. Pour in a little of the olive oil and pound it to a pulp. Gradually add the basil leaves and cheese with the rest of the oil, pounding all the time. You should have a thick paste.

Dice the Mozzarella. Peel the tomatoes by immersing them in boiling water until their skins burst. Chop them roughly. Mix the cheese, tomatoes and olives together and season.

Cook the pasta in boiling salted water, to which you have added a little olive oil, until *al dente*. Drain. Toss the pasta in the dressing. Pile it into four warmed serving bowls and top with the salad.

▲ ◄ Spaghetti with fresh tomato and basil Sauce

Chicory Soufflé

INGREDIENTS *serves 4-6*

3 heads chicory
salt
juice 1 lemon
3 tbsp/40g/1½oz butter
⅜ cup/40g/1½oz flour
1¼ cups/300ml/10fl oz milk
½ cup/50g/2oz grated cheese
4 eggs, separated
1 tbsp/15ml dry brown breadcrumbs

METHOD

Heat the oven to 400°F/200°C/Gas 6. Trim the chicory and cook in salted water to which you have added the lemon juice. This will stop it discolouring.

When the chicory is tender, drain and set aside. When it is cool, press the water out from between the leaves with your fingers. Chop the chicory very finely.

Meanwhile, melt the butter in a heavy-bottomed pan. Stir in the flour. Remove from the heat and stir in the milk. Return from the heat and stir until the sauce has thickened. Add the cheese and cook for a further minute. Allow to cool.

When the sauce has cooled, mix in the chicory, then the egg yolks.

Whisk the whites until they form soft peaks and fold into the chicory mixture. Spoon into a greased soufflé dish and sprinkle the top with breadcrumbs.

Bake in the oven for 20-25 minutes until lightly set, well risen and golden on top. Serve this soufflé with a strongly flavoured salad, such as watercress garnished with slivers of orange.

23

Flageolet and Sage Derby Quiche

INGREDIENTS *serves 4-6*
6oz/175g shortcrust pastry (enough for a single-crust pie)
4 large tomatoes
4oz/100g Sage Derby cheese
3 eggs
$^2/_3$ cup/150ml/5fl oz milk
salt and freshly ground black pepper
1 cup/175g/6oz flageolet beans, pre-soaked and cooked

METHOD
Pre-heat the oven to 400°F/200°C/Gas 6. Pour boiling water over the tomatoes. After a minute the skins will begin to split. Refresh with cold water. Peel the tomatoes and slice them thickly.

Line a 8in/22cm quiche pan with the pastry and crumble the cheese into it. Arrange the tomato slices to cover the cheese.

Break the eggs into a bowl and lightly beat with the milk and seasoning. Pour egg mixture into the pie crust, gently pressing down the tomatoes with a fork.

Bake in the centre of the oven for 15-20 minutes, until set and golden.

Onion Tart

INGREDIENTS *serves 4-6*
6oz/175g pastry (enough for a single-crust pie)
1 tbsp/15g/½oz butter
1 tbsp/15ml oil
2½ cups/550g/1lb 2oz finely chopped onions
2 eggs plus 1 yolk
2 cups/450ml/¾pt single cream
1-2 heaped tbsp/15-30ml grated Cheddar cheese
1-2 heaped tbsp/15-30ml chopped parsley
salt and freshly ground black pepper
pinch of cayenne pepper

METHOD
Heat the oven to 375°F/190°C/Gas 5 and line a 22cm/8in quiche pan with the pastry.

Heat the butter and olive oil in a pan. Stir in the onions. Cover the pan, turn down the heat and sweat for about 5 minutes, stirring occasionally until soft and transparent.

Beat the eggs, cream and cheese together and add the onions and parsley. Season with salt, pepper and cayenne to taste, pour into the pastry crust and bake in the middle of the oven for 30-40 minutes until golden and set.

VARIATION
To make an onion and blue cheese tart, combine 1-2 tbsp crumbled blue cheese with the cream before beating it with the eggs. Omit the Cheddar, parsley and cayenne pepper.

◀ Onion tart

24

Mushroom and Broccoli Nut Loaf

INGREDIENTS *serves 6*

³/₄ cup/50g/2oz sliced button
   mushrooms
2 tbsp/25g/1oz polyunsaturated
   margarine
2 stalks celery, chopped
1 clove garlic, crushed
1 onion, grated
1 tbsp/15ml wholemeal flour
1¹/₂ cups/400g/15oz can chopped
   tomatoes
2 cups/100g/4oz wholemeal
   breadcrumbs
1 cup/100g/4oz ground walnuts
1 egg
1 tsp/5ml fresh basil, chopped
1 tsp/5ml fresh oregano, chopped
1 tbsp/15ml parsley, chopped
salt and freshly ground black pepper
4oz/100g broccoli spears, cooked

SAUCE

1 cup/50g/2oz chopped mushrooms
3 tbsp/20g/³/₄oz wholemeal flour
¹/₂ cup/120ml/4fl oz vegetable stock
¹/₂ cup/120ml/4fl oz skimmed milk
celery leaves

METHOD

Sauté the mushroom slices in a frying pan with 1 tbsp/15g/¹/₂oz margarine, drain and place in a line down the centre of a lightly greased 2pt/1.1l loaf tin.

Cook the celery, garlic and onion in the pan until softened.

Stir in the flour and tomatoes and stir until thickened.

Add the breadcrumbs, nuts, egg, herbs and seasoning. Place half in the tin. Add the broccoli spears and top with the remaining mixture.

Cover with foil, place in a roasting pan filled with boiling water and cook at 350°F/180°C/Gas 4 for 1¹/₄-1¹/₂ hours.

Melt the remaining margarine, add the chopped mushrooms and cook for 2-3 minutes. Stir in the flour, and cook for 1 minute.

Add the stock, milk and seasoning and stir until boiled.

Turn out the loaf, garnish with celery leaves and serve with the sauce separately.

Summer Vegetable Pasties

INGREDIENTS *makes 4*
1 recipe Wholewheat Pastry
beaten egg to glaze

FILLING

1 cup/100g/4oz potatoes, diced
4 baby carrots, sliced
¹/₄ cup/50g/2oz garden peas
2 baby courgettes, sliced
2 stalks celery, sliced
¹/₂ green pepper, diced

CHEESE SAUCE

2 tbsp/25g/1oz butter
4 tbsp/25g/1oz untreated (unbleached)
   white flour
up to 1¹/₄ cups/300ml/¹/₂pt milk
¹/₂ cup/50g/2oz Cheddar cheese, grated
salt and freshly ground black pepper

METHOD

Make the pastry. Pre-heat the oven to 350°F/180°C/Gas 4.

Boil the potatoes and carrots in salted water until just tender. In another pan, boil the remaining vegetables for about 2 minutes. Drain.

To make the cheese sauce, melt the butter in a heavy-bottomed pan, stir in the flour and gradually add half the milk, stirring. Add the cheese. Stir until melted. Add a little more milk and season to taste. Don't make the sauce too thin or it will pour out of the pastry shells. Mix sauce into vegetables to coat them generously.

Divide the pastry into 4 balls and roll out. Share the mixture between the pastry rounds. Crimp together to form pasties and brush with beaten egg. Put the pasties on a baking tray and bake in the oven for 30 minutes or until the pastry is cooked.

Sabzi Vegetable Cutlet

INGREDIENTS *serves 4-6*
1 cup/100g/4oz beetroot, diced
1 cup/100g/4oz carrots, diced
2 cups/225g/8oz potatoes, diced
1¹/₂ cups/100g/4oz cabbage, shredded
¹/₂ tsp/2.5ml chilli powder
¹/₂ tsp/2.5ml ground roasted cumin
salt and freshly ground black pepper
Large pinch sugar
1 tbsp/15ml raisins (optional)
¹/₂ cup/50g/2oz flour
¹/₂ cup/120ml/4oz milk
breadcrumbs
oil for deep frying

METHOD
Boil the beetroot, carrots, potatoes and cabbage together until tender. Drain.

Mash the boiled vegetables with the chilli, roasted cumin, black pepper, salt, sugar and raisins. Divide into 12 balls and flatten. Chill for 1 hour.

Make a batter with the flour and milk and dip a cutlet in it. Then roll it in breadcrumbs until well coated.

Heat the oil in a large frying pan and fry the cutlets for 2-3 minutes turning once, until crisp and golden. Serve with coriander chutney.

Azuki Bean Burgers

INGREDIENTS *serves 4*
1 cup/450g/8oz azuki beans
bay leaf
2 onions, chopped
3 cloves garlic, chopped
1-2 tbsp/15-30ml oil
4 carrots, peeled and grated
juice 1 lemon
4 tbsp/60ml parsley, chopped
salt and freshly ground black pepper
soy sauce to taste
beaten egg for binding
wholewheat flour for coating

METHOD
Soak the azuki beans overnight. Drain, then cook until tender in fresh water with a bay leaf added. Drain, reserving the liquid.

Fry the onion and garlic in oil until transparent. Add the carrot and lemon juice and sweat, covered, until soft.

Add the beans, mix well and purée in a blender, adding a little of the bean liquor if necessary to form a malleable consistency. Stir in the parsley, season and add soy sauce to taste. Stir in enough beaten egg to bind.

Form into balls or burgers, coat with flour and shallow fry until brown and crispy on the outside. Serve with homemade Marinara Sauce.

▼ Sabzi vegetable cutlets

Kidney Bean, Artichoke and Mushroom Casserole

INGREDIENTS *serves 4*

1 cup/225g/8oz kidney beans
1-2 tbsp/15-30ml oil
1 large onion, chopped
1-2 cloves garlic, chopped
3 cups/175g/6oz mushrooms, sliced
1 cup/100g/4oz French beans, trimmed,
  cut in thirds and parboiled
1¾ cups/425g/15oz can artichoke
  hearts, drained
1¾ cups/425g/15oz can tomatoes,
  mashed
salt and freshly ground black pepper
parsley

METHOD

Soak the kidney beans overnight and cook until tender.

Pre-heat the oven to 350°F/180°C/Gas 4. Heat oil and fry onion and garlic until translucent. Add the mushrooms and stir-fry for 1-2 minutes until just soft.

Transfer all the ingredients to a casserole. Season well. Cover and bake for 30-40 minutes. Sprinkle with parsley and serve.

Bean Moussaka

INGREDIENTS *serves 4*

1 cup/225g/8oz rose cocoa beans
1 large aubergine, thinly sliced
oil
1 large onion, chopped
2 cloves garlic, chopped
1¾ cups/425g/15oz can tomatoes,
  mashed
1 tbsp/15ml tomato purée
2 tsp/10ml fresh thyme, chopped
salt and freshly ground black pepper

CHEESE SAUCE

2 tbsp/25g/1oz butter
4 tbsp/25g/1oz flour
1¼ cups/300ml/½pt milk
½ cup/50g/2oz grated Cheddar cheese
grated nutmeg to taste
salt and freshly ground black pepper

METHOD

Soak the beans overnight and cook until you can mash them with a fork. Drain.

Heat the oven to 350°F/180°C/Gas 4. Sprinkle the aubergine slices with salt and allow to stand in a colander for 30 minutes. Rinse and pat dry with kitchen paper. Heat some oil in a pan and fry aubergines gently until cooked. Set aside.

Add some more oil to the pan and fry the onion and garlic until translucent. Add the tomatoes, tomato purée, thyme and seasoning, and heat through, stirring. Mix in the beans. Set aside.

To make the cheese sauce, melt the butter in a thick-bottomed saucepan. Stir in the flour, then gradually add the milk, stirring all the time, until the sauce bubbles and thickens. Turn down the heat, add the cheese and stir till melted. Season with nutmeg and add salt and pepper to taste.

To assemble the dish, spread a layer of the bean mixture in the bottom of a casserole and top with aubergine slices. Spread thinly with cheese sauce. Continue to layer the ingredients until they are all used up, ending with a thick layer of the sauce. Bake in the oven to heat right through for 30-40 minutes and serve with a crisp green salad.

▼ Kidney bean, artichoke and mushroom casserole

Savoury Stuffed Vine Leaves

INGREDIENTS *serves 4*
1 cup/225g/8oz brown rice
olive oil
1 small onion, chopped
2 cloves garlic, chopped
salt and freshly ground black pepper
8oz/225g peeled bottled or canned
   chestnuts
1-2 tbsp/15-30ml butter
4oz/100g mushrooms
2 tomatoes, peeled and chopped
1tsp/5ml dried mixed herbs
20 vine leaves

METHOD
Wash the rice in several changes of cold water. Heat 1 tbsp/15ml oil in a heavy-bottomed pan and fry the onion and garlic until translucent. Stir in the rice and cook for a few minutes before covering with boiling water. (Use about ²/₃ water to ¹/₃ rice by volume.) Bring back to the boil, then cover the pan and turn the heat down very low. The rice should be cooked in about 40 minutes.

Meanwhile, drain the chestnuts and chop them finely. Heat the butter in a pan and add the mushrooms. When they are tender, add the tomatoes, chestnuts and herbs. Stir once or twice and remove from the heat.

When the rice is cooked, mix it thoroughly with the nut stuffing and check the seasoning. Use it, by the spoonful, to stuff the vine leaves. Pack them into an ovenproof dish, brush with olive oil and cover the dish with foil. Heat through in the oven. Stuffed vine leaves are best eaten hot, but they're good cold too, if you have any left over.

Bulghar Wheat Stuffed Peppers

INGREDIENTS *serves 4*
5oz/150g bulghar wheat
2 red peppers, cut in half lengthways
   and seeded
2 yellow peppers, cut in half lengthways
   and seeded
1 tbsp/15ml sunflower oil
1 onion, chopped
¹/₂ cup/50g/2oz chopped hazelnuts
²/₃ cup/75g/3oz chopped dried apricots
¹/₂tsp/2.5ml powdered ginger
1tsp/5ml cardamon seeds, ground
2 tbsp/30ml coriander leaves, finely
   chopped
3 tbsp/45ml natural yoghurt
fresh coriander leaves

METHOD
Place the bulghar wheat in a bowl, pour over 1¹/₄ cups/300ml/¹/₂pt boiling water and leave to stand for 15 minutes.

Place the peppers in a shallow, lightly oiled ovenproof dish.

Place the remaining oil in a saucepan, add the onion and gently fry until softened.

Stir in the bulghar wheat, hazelnuts, apricots, ginger and cardamon. Cook for 1 minute, stirring continuously.

Add the coriander and yoghurt, mix together and use to fill the pepper shells. Cover the dish tightly with aluminium foil and bake in a pre-heated oven at 375°F/190°C/Gas 5 for 30-35 minutes.

Serve immediately, garnished with coriander leaves.

Potato Topped Vegetable Pie

INGREDIENTS *serves 4-6*
½ cup/75g/3oz green lentils
¼ cup/50g/2oz pot barley
1 onion, chopped
1¾ cups/425ml/15oz can chopped
    tomatoes
6oz/175g cauliflower florets
2 stalks celery, sliced
1 leek, thickly sliced
1 turnip, sliced
2 carrots, diced
2 tbsp/30ml fresh mixed herbs, chopped
1½lb/750g potatoes, scrubbed
3 tbsp/45ml semi-skimmed milk
salt and freshly ground black pepper
2 tbsp/25g/1oz grated reduced fat
    medium hard cheese

METHOD
Place the lentils, barley, onion, tomatoes, cauliflower, celery, leek, turnip, carrots and herbs in a large saucepan with 1¼ cups/ 300ml/½pt water.

Bring to the boil, cover and simmer for 40-45 minutes or until everything is soft.

Cover potatoes with boiling water and cook for about 15 minutes, or until soft.

Drain, peel and mash the potatoes with the milk and season to taste.

Place the lentil mix in a pie dish and either pipe or fork the potato on top.

Sprinkle with cheese and place in a pre-heated oven at 400°F/200°C/Gas 6 for 30-35 minutes.

Wicklow "Pancakes"

INGREDIENTS *serves 4*
2 medium onions, sliced
1½lb/675g potatoes, sliced
6 tbsp/90ml olive oil
salt and black pepper
6 eggs
parsley

METHOD
Blanch the potatoes, then fry with the onions in the olive oil until they are very well cooked – do try not to brown either the onions or the potatoes. Drain off the excess oil, season to taste.

Whisk the eggs in a large bowl, then add the potato and onion mixture, along with some chopped parsley. Put a little oil in a pan and pour some of the mixture in until it is nearly 1in/2.5cm thick.

Cook over a moderate heat until reasonably firm, then turn over with the help of a dinner plate. Cook for a few minutes and turn out.

Cut into wedges and eat hot or cold.

Avocado Soufflé Omelette

INGREDIENTS *serves 2*
1 green pepper
3 tbsp/40g/1½oz butter
1 ripe avocado
dash lemon juice
4 eggs, separated
salt and freshly ground black pepper

METHOD
De-seed and slice the green pepper. Heat a little of the butter in a pan and fry gently until soft. Set aside.

Cut the avocado in half. Remove the stone and remove the flesh from the shell in one careful movement with a palette knife. Slice the avocado and sprinkle with lemon juice.

Beat the egg yolks and season with salt and pepper. Whisk the whites and fold the two together.

Heat half the remaining butter in a pan and pour in half the omelette mixture. Arrange half the avocado and green pepper on one side of it. When lightly set, fold the omelette in two, slide out of the pan and keep hot until you have made the second omelette in the same way.

◀▲ Wicklow "pancakes"
▲ Avocado soufflé omelette

Leek and Stilton Bake

INGREDIENTS *serves 4*
1lb/450g small leeks
6 eggs
1 slice wholewheat bread, crumbed
2 tbsp/30ml cider vinegar
4oz/100g Stilton cheese

METHOD
Pre-heat the oven to 400°F/200°C/Gas 6. Trim and wash the leeks. Steam for 10-15 minutes. Lay them in a greased ovenproof dish.

Beat the eggs with the vinegar and breadcrumbs and crumble in the Stilton. Pour over the leeks and bake for 30 minutes until risen and golden.

Eggs with Curly Kale

INGREDIENTS *serves 2-4*
1lb/450g curly kale
4 eggs
2tbsp/25g/1oz butter
¼ cup/25g/1oz plain untreated flour
1¼ cups/300ml/10fl oz milk
½ cup/50g/2oz Cheddar cheese, grated
salt and freshly ground black pepper

METHOD
Wash the kale and discard the stalks. Pack into a saucepan with a very little water, cover and cook slowly for about 20 minutes until tender. Drain and cut up roughly with a knife and fork. Put the kale in the bottom of

a heatproof serving dish and keep warm.
Soft-boil the eggs.

Meanwhile, make the cheese sauce. Melt the butter in a pan and stir in the flour. Cook, stirring for a few minutes. Gradually add the milk. Continue to stir until the sauce has thickened. Add the cheese. When it melts, season.

Plunge the eggs in cold water and remove the shells. Lay them on the bed of kale and cover with the sauce. Heat the dish through in the oven or under the grill.

Cheese Strudel

INGREDIENTS *serves 4*
12oz/350g packet puff pastry
1½ cups/175g/6oz grated Cheddar cheese
⅔ cup/100g/4oz cream cheese
⅔ cup/100g/4oz curd cheese
1 egg
chopped parsley or mint
salt and freshly ground black pepper
egg white for glazing

METHOD
Roll the pastry out as thinly as possible.

Mix the remaining ingredients except the egg white until smooth. Spread the mixture over the pastry.

Fold over to make a flattish strip, sealing the edges well. Brush with the egg white. Place on a moistened baking sheet and bake at 400°F/200°C/Gas 6 for 20 minutes.

Serve hot, with soured cream if liked.

Broccoli and Tomato Cheesecake

INGREDIENTS *serves 4-6*
1 cup/100g/4oz wholewheat biscuit (cracker) crumbs
4tbsp/50g/2oz butter, softened

THE FILLING
8oz/250g broccoli florets
1 large tomato
1½ cups/350g/12oz curd cheese
salt and freshly ground white pepper
pinch nutmeg
2 eggs, separated

THE TOPPING
broccoli florets

METHOD
Pre-heat the oven to 350°F/180°C//Gas 4. Combine the crumbs and the butter and press down well into a greased 8in/22cm quiche pan with a loose bottom.

Steam the broccoli florets over boiling salted water until tender. Carefully slice some of the florets for decorating and reserve the rest. Immerse the tomato in boiling water for a minute, refresh in cold water, peel and de-seed.

Mash the curd cheese with the broccoli and tomato and season well with salt, pepper and a good pinch of nutmeg. Beat in the egg yolks.

Whisk the whites until they form soft peaks and fold into the mixture. Pour the filling over the crumb base and bake for about 20-25 minutes until slightly risen and just set.

Allow to cool. When cold, remove the sides of the tin and decorate the top with the remaining broccoli florets. Chill before serving.

◀▲ Leek and Stilton bake

Courgettes with Almonds

INGREDIENTS *serves 4*
6 large/700g/1½lb courgettes, sliced
    lengthways
1 medium onion, finely chopped
1 tbsp/15ml olive oil
salt and freshly ground black pepper
⅓ cup/50g/2oz flaked almonds
1 tsp/5ml cornstarch
1 tbsp/15ml water
1 cup/250ml/8fl oz yoghurt

METHOD
Place the courgettes in a shallow ovenproof
dish. Mix the onions, oil, salt and pepper
and spoon the mixture over the courgettes.
Bake uncovered at 350°F/180°C/Gas 4 for
40 minutes, or until tender.

Meanwhile toast the almonds: put them
into a heavy frying pan over a high heat and
shake the pan frequently; don't burn.

Mix the cornstarch with the water and
add it to the yoghurt with seasoning to taste.

Warm the mixture over a gentle heat,
stirring constantly, for 3 minutes.

Spoon it over the courgettes and scatter
the almonds on top.

Courgette Gratin

INGREDIENTS *serves 4*
oil
4 large/450g/1lb courgettes, sliced
1 large onion, chopped
1¾ cups/425g/15oz canned tomatoes
chopped basil, thyme or marjoram
sliver lemon peel
salt and freshly ground black pepper
1 cup/225g/8oz macaroni
2 eggs
⅔ cup/150ml/¼pt yoghurt
¾ cup/75g/3oz grated Cheddar cheese

METHOD
Heat the oil and fry the courgettes until they
are lightly coloured. Remove them from the

pan and reserve. Add the onion and fry until
golden, adding more oil if necessary. Add
the tomatoes, herbs, lemon peel, salt and
pepper and simmer for 10 minutes,
breaking up the tomatoes and stirring from
time to time.

Meanwhile, cook the macaroni and
drain it well. Put it into an ovenproof dish.

Pour the sauce over the macaroni and mix
it through well. Lay the cooked courgettes
on top. Mix the eggs, yoghurt and half the
cheese and pour the mixture over the
courgettes. Scatter the remaining cheese on
top.

Bake the dish at 375°F/190°C/Gas 5 for
30 minutes.

VARIATION
You could use aubergines instead of
courgettes, in which case slice and salt
them, leave them to drain for 20 minutes,
rinse and dry them and proceed as above.

▼ Courgette gratin

Chilli Beans

INGREDIENTS *serves 4*
1 cup/175g/6oz rose cocoa beans
2 tbsp/30ml olive oil
¹/₂ tsp/2.5g fennel seeds
¹/₂ tsp/2.5g mustard seeds
1 onion, chopped
2 cloves garlic, chopped
1¾ cup/100g/4oz sliced mushrooms
¹/₂ fresh green chilli, de-seeded and
    chopped
1¾ cups/425g/15oz can tomatoes,
    mashed
2 tbsp/30ml chopped fresh coriander or
    parsley
salt and freshly ground black pepper

METHOD
Soak the beans overnight and cook them in salted water until tender. Cooking time will vary depending on the age of the beans. They could be ready in 20 minutes, or they may take an hour, so keep testing.

Meanwhile, heat the oil in a pan and, when hot, add the seeds. As soon as the mustard seeds begin to pop, add the onion and garlic. Cook gently until translucent.

Stir in the mushrooms. When they are tender, add the chilli and tomatoes, coriander and seasoning. If you can't get coriander, use parsley instead, but the dish will certainly lose some of its character.

Add the beans, heat through for 10 minutes and serve with toasted rarebit or an omelette for a warming winter supper.

Courgettes with Dill

INGREDIENTS *serves 4*
¹/₄ cup/60ml/2fl oz olive oil
2 tbsp/25g/1oz butter
1 onion, chopped
1 garlic, crushed
450g/1lb courgettes topped, tailed and
    sliced in thickish rounds
salt and freshly ground black pepper
2 tsp/10ml paprika
1 tbsp/15ml dill, chopped (not the
    stalks)
1 small tub soured cream

METHOD
Heat oil and butter in a large frying pan. Cook the onion and garlic gently until soft. Turn up the heat.

Add the courgettes, garlic and black pepper and toss.

Cook for 5-10 minutes, stirring to cook both sides of the courgette slices.

When browning, add the paprika, dill and soured cream. Season and serve.

Magyar Marrow or Squash

INGREDIENTS *serves 4*
1 medium to large marrow
2 tbsp/25g/1oz butter
2 tsp/10ml cornflour
1 tbsp/15ml water
1 tbsp/15ml dried dill weed
salt and freshly ground black pepper
²/₃ cup/150ml/¹/₄pt soured cream

METHOD
Peel the marrow and either finely chop or grate it. Cook the marrow with the butter, stirring from time to time, just until it begins to soften. Mix the cornflour with the water until smooth and add it to the marrow. Stir and cook for a further 3 minutes. Add the dill, salt and pepper and finally stir in the soured cream. Warm it through gently and serve the marrow hot.

▲ Courgettes with dill
► Chilli beans

Stuffed Marrow or Squash

INGREDIENTS *serves 4-6*
1 marrow
salt and freshly ground black pepper
1/3 cup/75g/3oz brown rice
2 small carrots, diced
1/4 cup/50g/2oz peas
1-2 tbsp/15-30ml oil
1 onion, chopped
1 clove garlic, chopped
1 stalk celery, chopped
1 handful parsley, chopped
2 tbsp hazelnuts, chopped

TOMATO SAUCE
1-2 tbsp/15-30ml oil
1 onion, chopped
2 cloves garlic, chopped
1¾ cups/425g/15oz can tomatoes,
    mashed
1 tbsp/15ml tomato purée
salt and freshly ground black pepper

METHOD
Pre-heat the oven to 350°F/180°C/Gas 4. Cut the marrow in half lengthways and scoop out the pith and seeds. Sprinkle the flesh with salt and leave the halves upside down to drain.

Meanwhile, make the filling. Simmer the rice in a covered pan of salted water until just tender (about 30 minutes). Drain.

Parboil carrots and peas and drain. Heat oil in a pan and fry onion and garlic until translucent. Add celery, carrots and peas. Stir in the rice, parsley and hazelnuts and season well. Dry the marrow and pile filling into one half of it. Top with second half.

Make the tomato sauce. Heat oil in a pan and add onion and garlic. Fry, stirring, until soft. Add tomatoes and tomato purée. Simmer for 5 minutes stirring occasionally, and season well.

Place marrow in a baking dish with a lid, if you have one big enough, otherwise use foil to cover. Surround it with the sauce. Cover and cook for 45 minutes until marrow is tender. Serve hot or cold with a crisp green salad.

Creamed Spinach

INGREDIENTS *serves 4*
3 cups/700g/1½lb fresh spinach, washed
    and picked over
1 egg yolk
grated nutmeg
salt and freshly ground black pepper
2/3 cup/150ml/1/4pt yoghurt

METHOD
Cook the spinach without any excess water (the water adhering to it is sufficient) and a little salt. Drain the cooked spinach very well (press it between two plates for most effective drainage).

Whisk together the egg yolk, nutmeg and seasoning to taste, and yoghurt. Mix into the spinach. Warm through gently.

NOTE
If you prefer to use frozen spinach, use leaf, not chopped spinach.

Roasted Aubergine

INGREDIENTS *serves 4*
1 large aubergine
1 small onion, finely chopped
1-2 green chillis, finely chopped
½ tsp/2.5ml salt
2-3 tbsp/30-45ml mustard oil

METHOD
Place the aubergine under a pre-heated grill for about 15 minutes, turning frequently, until the skin becomes black and the flesh soft.

Peel the skin and mash the flesh.

Add the rest of the ingredients to the mashed aubergine and mix thoroughly.

Brussels Sprouts with Garlic and Mushrooms

INGREDIENTS *serves 4*
2-3 tbsp/30-45ml oil
4 cloves garlic, chopped
1lb/450g Brussels sprouts, thinly sliced
1¼ cups/100g/4oz mushrooms, sliced

METHOD
Heat some oil in a wok or deep-sided frying pan. Add the garlic and fry quickly, stirring, until crisp and brown.

Add the sprouts and mushrooms and stir until coated with garlic and oil. Stir-fry for 1-2 minutes and eat while crisp and hot. A delicious accompaniment to bean dishes.

Cauliflower with Potatoes and Peas

INGREDIENTS *serves 4-6*
4 tbsp/60ml oil
2 medium onions, finely chopped
4 cups/450g/1lb diced potatoes in ¾in/2cm pieces
1 small cauliflower, cut into ¾in/2cm pieces
½ tsp/2.5ml ground turmeric
⅓ tsp/3ml chilli powder
1 tsp/5ml ground cumin
2 tomatoes, chopped
1 tsp/5ml salt
¼ tsp/1.5ml sugar
1 cup/200g/7oz peas
½ tsp/2.5ml Garam Masala

METHOD
Heat the oil in a karai over medium high heat. Add the onions and fry for 3-4 minutes until light brown.

Add the potatoes and cauliflower and stir. Add the spices, tomatoes, salt and sugar. Stir and fry for 2-3 minutes.

Add the peas, cover and lower heat to medium low and cook for about 20 minutes until the potatoes and cauliflower are tender. Stir the vegetables a few times to stop them sticking. Sprinkle with Garam Masala before serving.

▲ ▶ Carrots with yoghurt
▶ Cauliflower with potatoes and peas

Carrots with Yoghurt

INGREDIENTS *serves 4-6*
3½ cups/450g/1lb carrots, sliced
1 tsp/5ml sugar
½ tsp/2.5ml ground cumin
1 small onion, finely chopped
juice ½ lemon
⅔ cup/150ml/¼pt yoghurt
salt and pepper

METHOD
Cook the carrots with the sugar in boiling water just until they are al dente. Drain them and add the cumin and onion. Stir around.

Mix the lemon juice into the yoghurt, season to taste and spoon it over the carrots.

Serve immediately or leave it to cool and serve as a salad or an accompaniment to curry.

Purée of Root Vegetables

INGREDIENTS *serves 4*
175g/6oz carrots
175g/6oz swede
1 turnip
1 parsnip
butter
salt and freshly ground black pepper

METHOD
Trim and peel the vegetables and simmer in salted water until tender.

Drain and mash to a fluffy purée with butter. Season with salt and plenty of black pepper. Serve with a dish that has a crunchy texture, such as Chestnuts and Vegetables.

Corn Croquettes

INGREDIENTS *serves 4*
3 tbsp/45ml butter
3 tbsp/20g/³/₄oz flour
1¼ cups/300ml/10fl oz milk
salt and freshly ground black pepper
1-2 tbsp/15-30ml finely chopped parsley
2¹/₃ cups/400g/14oz corn kernels, cooked
2 egg yolks

THE COATING
2 eggs, beaten
seasoned flour
fine stale breadcrumbs
oil for frying

METHOD
To make the sauce, cut the butter into small pieces and melt in a heavy-bottomed pan. Stir in the flour and cook for a few minutes until the mixture is a pale gold.

Remove from the heat and pour in the milk. Stir well, return to the heat and stir until the sauce has thickened. Season with salt and plenty of pepper.

Stir the parsley, corn kernels and egg yolks into the mixture. Chill.

The mixture should have a heavy dropping consistency. Form it into croquettes. Dip each in the beaten egg, then roll in the flour and breadcrumbs.

Fry the croquettes in oil until crisp.

Fennel Mornay

INGREDIENTS *serves 4*
3 bulbs fennel
bay leaf

THE SAUCE
2 tbsp/25g/1oz butter
¼ cup/25g/1oz plain untreated flour
1¼ cups/300ml/10fl oz milk
²/₃ cup/150ml/5fl oz single cream
1 cup/100g/4oz Cheddar cheese, grated
¼-¹/₂ cup/25-50g/1-2oz breadcrumbs
salt and freshly ground black pepper

METHOD
Trim the fennel and simmer in salted water with a bay leaf for about 30 minutes until tender.

Meanwhile, make the sauce. Melt the butter in a pan and stir in the flour. Cook, stirring, for a couple of minutes and then gradually stir in the milk. Add the cream and most of the cheese and cook gently until the cheese has melted. Season well and keep warm.

Drain the fennel and cut each bulb in half. Lay the halves in a flameproof dish and pour the sauce over them. Sprinkle with the remaining cheese and the breadcrumbs. Put under a hot grill to brown and melt the cheese.

NOTE
For a tangier sauce, add a little powdered English mustard to taste.

Corn on the Cob with Garlic Butter

INGREDIENTS *serves 4-6*
Corn on the cob
butter
garlic paste

METHOD
Remove the outer green leaves from the fresh corn. Place in boiling salted water with a drop of olive oil.

Simmer for 20 minutes, or until the corn is cooked and tender.

Remove from the heat and drain.

Smother liberally with butter and garlic paste.

Cheese and Potato Croquettes

INGREDIENTS *serves 6-8*
2lb/900g potatoes
2 egg yolks
4 tbsp/50g/2oz butter
salt and freshly ground black pepper
pinch nutmeg
dash sherry
½ cup/100g/4oz grated Parmesan
    cheese
pinch mustard
2 tbsp/30ml chopped parsley
seasoned flour
eggwash (egg beaten with a little milk)
breadcrumbs

METHOD
Wash and peel the potatoes, and cut to an even size. Cook in salted water until soft; then drain.

Put a lid on the pan of the potatoes and place over a low heat to dry out, stirring occasionally to prevent burning.

Place the potatoes in a food processor with the yolks, butter and seasoning.

Mix in the nutmeg, sherry, Parmesan cheese, mustard and parsley. The potatoes should be like a very firm mash. Overmixing will make them gluey, in which case some flour will have to be worked in by hand.

Check that the mix is seasoned well and mould into cylinder shapes (5×2in/13×5cm).

Roll in seasoned flour; dip in eggwash and coat with breadcrumbs.

Deep-fry in hot fat, 365°F/185°C. When golden, drain well and serve.

NOTE
If you want to keep the croquettes for cooking later, or the next day, place them carefully on a tray, cover with plastic film and refrigerate.

Split Peas with Vegetables

INGREDIENTS *serves 4-6*
scant cup/200g/7oz split peas, washed
3 cups/750ml/25fl oz water
2 tbsp/30ml Ghee
½ tsp/2.5ml whole cumin seeds
2 bay leaves
2-3 green chillis, cut lengthways
2½ cups/275g/10oz diced potatoes, cut
    into 1in/2.5cm pieces
⅓ cup/75g/3oz peas
3 cups/350g/12oz cauliflower, cut into
    large florets
½ tsp/2.5ml ground turmeric
1 tsp/5ml salt

METHOD
In a large saucepan bring the split peas and water to the boil. Cover and simmer for 30 minutes. Remove from heat.

Heat the ghee in a large saucepan over medium high heat. Add the cumin seeds, bay leaves and green chillis and let them sizzle for a few seconds.

Add the potatoes, peas, cauliflower and fry for 1-2 minutes.

Add the boiled split peas with the water, turmeric and salt. Mix thoroughly, lower heat and cook until the vegetables are tender. (If the dal gets too thick add a little more water.)

▶ ▲ Split peas with vegetables
▶ Corn on the cob with garlic butter

Black Eyed Peas with Onions

INGREDIENTS *serves 4-6*
1 good cup/200g/7oz black eyed peas, washed
5 cups/1.1l/2pts water
2 tbsp/30ml oil
1 large onion, finely chopped
2 cloves garlic, crushed
¼in/0.5cm root ginger, grated
1-2 green chillis, finely chopped
½ tsp/2.5ml salt
1 tsp/5ml molasses

METHOD
Soak the beans in the water overnight.

Boil the beans in the water and then cover and simmer for 1 hour until tender. Drain.

Heat the oil in a large saucepan and fry the onion, garlic, ginger and chilli until the onions are soft. Add the beans, salt and molasses and cook until all the moisture is absorbed, about 15 minutes. Serve with Baktoras.

Three Peppers in Tomato and Garlic

INGREDIENTS *serves 6*
¾ cup/175ml/6fl oz olive oil
2 yellow peppers, de-seeded and cut into thin strips
2 red peppers, de-seeded and vut into thin strips
2 green peppers, de-seeded and cut into thin strips
1 tbsp/15ml parsley, chopped
2 tsp/10ml finely chopped garlic
8oz/225g fresh or canned tomatoes
salt and freshly ground black pepper

METHOD
Heat the oil in a large frying pan and cook the peppers gently for 2-3 minutes, stirring frequently. Add the parsley and garlic and cook for another couple of minutes.

Add the chopped tomatoes and their juice to the pan. Stir and season.

Cover and simmer gently for about 20 minutes, until the peppers are tender.

The sauce should be quite thick - if necessary, remove the peppers and boil rapidly to reduce the liquid. Season.

▲ ▲ Black eyed peas with onions   ▲ Patatas bravas

Yoghurt

INGREDIENTS *makes about 5 cups*
5 cups/1.1l/2pts milk
2 tbsp/30ml unflavoured commercial
    yoghurt at room temperature

METHOD
Scald the milk. Heat it until it is ready to
boil. Just before boiling point, remove the
pan from the heat and allow to cool until
lukewarm. Test by dripping a little milk on
your wrist. It should feel warm, not hot.

    Put the yoghurt in the chosen container
and stir in a little milk until smooth. Now
stir in the remaining milk.

    Cover and place container in the
incubator. Be careful not to disturb the
yoghurt for about 4 hours. When the
consistency is right, chill in the fridge to set
before using.

NOTE
Yoghurt can be made in any sterile container
with a tightly fitting lid inside any sort of
incubator, such as an oven with the pilot
light on or a styrofoam box, but because the
secret of successful yoghurt making is a
constant lukewarm temperature, it is best to
use a special yoghurt maker. Don't put
incubating yoghurt near a heat source
regulated by a thermostat that switches on
and off. Use 2 tbsp/30ml of the home-made
yoghurt to start the next batch. The cost of
making yoghurt at home is minimal and the
method is easy.

Ghee-Clarified Butter

INGREDIENTS *makes about 2 cups/
450ml/³/₄pt*
1lb/450g unsalted butter

METHOD
Heat the butter in a saucepan over low heat.
Let it simmer for 15-20 minutes until all the
white residue turns golden and settles at the
bottom.

    Remove from the heat, strain and cool.

    Pour into an airtight bottle and store in a
cool place.

Homemade Garam Masala

INGREDIENTS *makes about ¹/₃ cup/2oz/
4 tbsp*
3 tbsp/45ml cardamom seeds
3in/7.5cm cinnamon sticks
¹/₂ tbsp/7.5ml cumin seeds
¹/₂ tsp/2.5ml black peppercorns
¹/₂ tsp/2.5ml cloves
¹/₄ nutmeg

METHOD
Grind all the spices together until they are
finely ground. Store in a spice bottle until
required. (The ingredients may be added in
different proportions to suit individual
tastes.)

Béchamel Sauce

INGREDIENTS *makes about 3³/₄ cups/
900ml/1¹/₂pts*
2¹/₂ cups/600ml/1pt milk
1 small onion, peeled
1 small carrot, peeled and sliced
1 bay leaf
6 slightly crushed peppercorns
1 blade mace
1 stalk parsley
3 tbsp/40g/1¹/₂oz butter
6 tbsp/40g/1¹/₂oz flour
salt and white pepper

METHOD
Pour milk into a saucepan. Add the onion
cut into quarters with 2 slices of carrot, bay
leaf, peppercorns, mace and parsley stalk.

    Cover and allow to heat on a low heat
without boiling for about 10 minutes.
Remove from the heat and allow to infuse
for a further 10 minutes, covered.

    Make a roux (a blend of butter and flour)
by melting the butter in a saucepan. Do not
allow the butter to brown. Add the flour and
stir well over a medium heat.

    Gradually add the strained milk and stir
briskly or whisk until a smooth creamy
sauce is made, season to taste.

Cold Horseradish Sauce

INGREDIENTS *makes about ¹/₄ cup/
200ml/7 fl oz*
2 tbsp/30ml prepared horseradish cream
²/₃ cup/150ml/¹/₄pt soured cream

METHOD
Stir the horseradish cream into the soured
cream. Refrigerate for an hour before use if
possible.

    Use this sauce for potatoes and beetroot
    dishes.

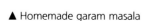

▲ Homemade garam masala

Creamy Mustard Vinaigrette

INGREDIENTS *makes about $^2/_3$ cup/ 150ml/$^1/_4$pt*
3 tbsp/45ml olive oil
2 tbsp/30ml double cream
2 tbsp/30ml red wine vinegar
1 tbsp/15ml Dijon mustard
$^1/_2$ tsp/2.5ml dried thyme
$1^1/_2$ tsp/7.5ml soy sauce
salt and freshly ground black pepper

METHOD
Put the olive oil, cream, vinegar and mustard in a small bowl. Stir with a fork or whisk until the mixture is just foamy. Stir in the thyme, soy sauce, salt and pepper.

Modern Vinaigrette

INGREDIENTS *makes 1 cup/250ml/ 8fl oz*
2 tbsp/30ml wine vinegar
1 tbsp/15ml lemon juice
1 tsp/5ml prepared mustard
salt and freshly ground black pepper
$^3/_4$ cup/175g/6fl oz pure olive oil
3 tsp/15ml mixed fresh herbs (optional)

METHOD
Put the vinegar, lemon juice, mustard, salt and pepper in a jar with a tightly fitting lid.

Cover the jar tightly and shake until the salt dissolves. Add the olive oil to the jar and shake until well mixed. Stir in the chopped basil, oregano or mix of herbs if wanted.

Tofu Dressing

INGREDIENTS *makes about 2 cups/ 475ml/16fl oz*
$1^2/_3$ cups/300g/10oz silken tofu
2 tbsp/30ml lemon juice
3 tbsp/45ml oil
pinch salt
1 tsp/5ml soy sauce
1 clove garlic, crushed

METHOD
Blend everything together in a liquidiser.

Mayonnaise

INGREDIENTS *makes 1$^1/_4$ cups/400ml/ 14fl oz*
2 egg yolks
$^1/_2$ tsp/2.5ml salt
1 tsp/5ml Dijon mustard
$1^1/_4$ cups/300ml/$^1/_2$pt olive oil
2 tsp/10ml cider vinegar

METHOD
All the ingredients must be at room temperature. Put the egg yolks in a bowl with the salt and mustard and whisk together with a balloon whisk.

Beating constantly and evenly, add the olive oil at a very slow trickle. A bottle with a nick cut in the cork can be used to ensure that only a very little oil dribbles out at a time. The aim is to break up the oil into very small globules so that it can be absorbed by the egg yolks. When all the oil has been added you should have a thick glossy emulsion that will cling to the whisk.

Gradually beat in the cider vinegar. For a thinner mayonnaise, beat in 1 tbsp/15ml hot water.

Mayonnaise Maltaise

INGREDIENTS *makes 1$^3/_4$ cups/400ml/ 14fl oz*
$1^3/_4$ cups/400ml/14fl oz mayonnaise (see above)
grated rind and juice of 2 oranges

METHOD
Combine the ingredients and serve with cooked vegetables such as asparagus and artichokes, or use as a salad dressing.

Blue Cheese Dressing

INGREDIENTS *makes about 1$^1/_4$ cups/ 400ml/14fl oz*
1 cup/250ml/8fl oz yoghurt
$^1/_2$ cup/50g/2oz blue cheese
3 tbsp/45ml olive oil
salt and freshly ground black pepper

METHOD
Blend all the ingredients together thoroughly.

Tomato Yoghurt Dressing

INGREDIENTS *makes $^3/_4$ cup/175ml/ 6fl oz*
$^2/_3$ cup/150ml/$^1/_4$pt yoghurt
4 tsp/20ml tomato ketchup
squeeze of lemon
dash Tabasco
salt and freshly ground black pepper

METHOD
Mix all the ingredients together well. Serve on crisp lettuce.

VARIATION
Add finely chopped green or red pepper, chopped hard-boiled egg, chopped spring onions.

Rich French Dressing

INGREDIENTS *makes about 1$^1/_4$ cups/ 400ml/14fl oz*
1 egg
$^1/_2$ cup/120ml/4fl oz oil
2 tbsp/30ml lemon juice
1 clove garlic, crushed
fresh herbs
salt and freshly ground black pepper
1 cup/250ml/8fl oz yoghurt

METHOD
Blend together the egg, oil, lemon juice, garlic, herbs, salt and pepper. Slowly add the yoghurt, with the blender running. Refrigerate until required - it should thicken as it stands.

VARIATION
This makes a delicious salad dressing but if you want to make it thicker, for piping, you can add some gelatin and let it set. Use chives, fennel, parsley, tarragon or any other fresh herb you have on hand - or a mixture.

NOTE
For a less rich dressing omit the egg.

Green Mayonnaise

INGREDIENTS *makes about 1½ cups/ 350ml/12fl oz*
3 tbsp/45ml chopped fresh spinach
3 tbsp/45ml chopped watercress
3 tbsp/45ml chopped spring onion
3 tbsp/45ml chopped parsley
1 cup/250ml/8fl oz mayonnaise
½ tsp/2.5g grated nutmeg
salt to taste

METHOD
Put the spinach, watercress, spring onion and parsley in a small saucepan. Add water to cover them.

Quickly bring to the boil. Remove the saucepan from the heat. Let stand for 1 minute.

Drain the greens well. Rub them through a sieve or purée them in a blender. Drain off excess liquid.

Put the mayonnaise in a blender or medium-sized bowl. Add the purée, nutmeg and salt to taste. Blend until evenly mixed.

Touch of Asia Dressing

INGREDIENTS *makes 1 cup/250ml/ 8fl oz*
2 tsp/10ml soy sauce
2 tsp/10ml water
1 whole spring onion, chopped
½ tsp/2.5ml sesame oil
¼ tsp/1.5ml hot pepper chilli oil
1 garlic clove, finely chopped
¼ tsp/1.5ml ground black pepper
6fl oz/175ml peanut oil
2½ tbsp/38ml rice wine vinegar

METHOD
Put the soy sauce, water, spring onion, sesame oil, hot pepper oil, garlic and black pepper in a jar with a tightly fitting lid. Cover and shake until the ingredients are blended.

Add the peanut oil to the jar, cover tightly and shake again. Let the mixture stand for 2 minutes.

Add the vinegar to the jar. Cover tightly and shake well again. Pour over the salad immediately.

Lemon Dressing

INGREDIENTS *makes ¾ cup/175ml/ 6fl oz*
1 tsp/5ml water
large pinch salt
large pinch grated lemon rind
2 tsp/10ml dried mint
4 tbsp/60ml/2fl oz fresh lemon juice
½ cup/120ml/4fl oz pure olive oil
large pinch ground black pepper

METHOD
Put the water, salt and lemon rind in a jar with a tightly fitting lid. Let stand for 2 minutes.

Add the mint and lemon juice. Cover the jar tightly and shake.

Add the olive oil and black pepper. Cover the jar tightly, shake again and serve.

Yoghurt Mayonnaise

INGREDIENTS *makes 1 cup/250ml/ 8fl oz*
½ cup/4fl oz/120ml unflavoured yoghurt
1 tbsp/15ml honey
1 tsp/5ml fresh lemon juice
4½ tbsp/3fl oz/90ml mayonnaise
¼ tsp/1.5ml salt
1 tsp/5ml poppy seeds

METHOD
Combine the yoghurt, honey and lemon juice in a bowl. Stir with a wooden spoon until well blended.

Add the mayonnaise, salt and poppy seeds. Stir until thoroughly mixed. Chill for 1 hour and serve.

Basil Dressing

INGREDIENTS *makes 1 cup/250ml/ 8fl oz*
1 cup/250ml/8fl oz yoghurt
10 basil leaves, finely chopped
1 large clove garlic, crushed
salt and freshly ground black pepper

METHOD
Blend everything together well. Serve over green or mixed salad or tomato and onion salad.

NOTE
This also makes a good sauce for pasta, in which case double the quantity.

Herb Dressing

INGREDIENTS *makes 1½ cups/350ml/ 12fl oz*
½ cup/75g/3oz cream cheese
1 cup/250ml/8fl oz yoghurt or buttermilk
salt and freshly ground black pepper
finely chopped fresh herbs

METHOD
Blend everything together well. Refrigerate until required. Use on salads or fish.

Tahini Dressing

INGREDIENTS *makes 1¼ cups/400ml/ 14fl oz*
1 cup/250ml/8fl oz tahini
4 tbsp/60ml water
4 tbsp/60ml lemon juice
3 cloves garlic, crushed
pinch salt

METHOD
Blend all the ingredients together thoroughly.

Thousand Island Dressing

INGREDIENTS *makes 1¹/₃ cups/325ml/ 11fl oz*
1 cup/250ml/8fl oz mayonnaise
4 tbsp/60ml Tabasco or chilli sauce
2 tbsp/30ml finely chopped pimento-
    stuffed green olives
1 hard-boiled egg, finely chopped
1 tbsp/15ml double cream
¹/₂ tsp/2.5ml fresh lemon juice
1¹/₂ tsp/7.5ml finely chopped spring
    onion
2 tbsp/30ml finely chopped sweet green
    pepper
2 tbsp/30ml finely chopped fresh parsley
¹/₄ tsp/1.5ml paprika
large pinch freshly ground black pepper

METHOD
Put the mayonnaise and chilli sauce in a medium-sized bowl. Stir with a wooden spoon until well blended.

Add the olives, egg, cream and lemon juice. Continue stirring.

Add the remaining ingredients. Stir until well blended. Refrigerate for at least 1 hour before serving. It goes well on tossed green salad.

Chutney Dressing

INGREDIENTS *makes about 1¹/₂ cups/ 350ml/12fl oz*
¹/₂ cup/120ml/4fl oz soured cream
¹/₂ cup/120ml/4fl oz buttermilk
2 tbsp/30ml mango chutney
1 tbsp/15ml lemon juice
2 tsp/10ml oil
2 tsp/10ml mustard
salt and freshly ground black pepper

METHOD
Blend everything together well. Refrigerate until required.

Serve on salad or cold vegetables. It also makes a delicious dressing for hard-cooked eggs.

Fruit Salad Syrup Dressing

INGREDIENTS *makes 1¹/₄ cups/300ml/ ¹/₂pt*
1 tbsp/15ml flour
²/₃ cup/150ml/¹/₄pt water
¹/₂ tsp/2.5ml pure vanilla essence
1 egg
5 tbsp/75ml sugar
2 tsp/10ml butter
large pinch ground nutmeg
3 tbsp/45ml double cream

METHOD
Put the flour and 2 tbsp/30ml water into a saucepan. Stir to form a thin paste. Add the vanilla and egg. Beat well until smooth.

Put the sugar, remaining water and butter in another saucepan. Bring to the boil over a low heat.

Add the boiling syrup to the vanilla and egg mixture. Stir well. Cook over low heat, stirring constantly, until thick and smooth.

Remove the saucepan from the heat. Allow the dressing to cool.

Stir in the nutmeg and cream. Beat until well blended and pour over the fruit salad.

Salsa Verde

INGREDIENTS *makes about 1¹/₂ cups/ 350ml/12fl oz*
3 cloves of garlic, finely chopped
1 cup/100g/4oz parsley, finely chopped
1 tbsp/15g watercress leaves, finely
    chopped (optional)
1 tbsp/15g mixed fresh herbs, finely
    chopped (basil, marjoram, and a little
    thyme, sage, chervil and dill)
coarse salt
4 tbsp/60ml olive oil
juice of 1-2 lemons
1-2 tsp/5-10g sugar
black pepper

METHOD
Blend or pound together in a mortar, the garlic, parsley, watercress, fresh mixed herbs and a little coarse salt, until they form a smooth paste.

Add the oil, a spoonful at a time, and mix well. Add the lemon juice and season with sugar, salt and pepper to taste. This goes excellently with hard-boiled eggs or fritters.

▲ Thousand island dressing

Hazelnut and Apricot Crunch

INGREDIENTS *makes about 16*
8 tbsp/100g/4oz butter
⅓ cup/50g/2oz soft brown sugar
2 tbsp/30ml maple syrup
1⅓ cups/100g/4oz porridge (rolled) oats
½ cup/50g/2oz chopped hazelnuts
⅓ cup/50g/2oz dried apricots, chopped

METHOD
Pre-heat the oven to 350°F/180°C/Gas 4. Put the butter, sugar and syrup in a heavy pan and stir over a low heat until combined.

Stir in the remaining ingredients. Press into a Swiss roll pan lined with greaseproof paper. Bake for about 45 minutes, until golden. Cut into bars in the pan using an oiled knife. Cool in the tin.

Amarett Biscuits

INGREDIENTS *makes about 20*
2 egg whites
½ cup/100g/4oz fruit sugar
⅔ cup/100g/4oz ground almonds
1 tsp/5ml kirsch (optional)
few drops vanilla essence
almond slivers for decorating

METHOD
Pre-heat the oven to 350°F/180°C/Gas 4. Whisk the egg whites until they form soft peaks. Gradually add the sugar, whisking continuously until the mixture is thick and lustrous. Stir in the ground almonds, kirsch and vanilla.

Line baking sheets with sheets of rice paper. Take a spoonful of mixture about the size of a plum and roll it into a ball in the palms of your hands. With a sticky mixture, you will find it easier if your hands are wet. Flatten the balls and arrange them on the baking trays with plenty of space for them to expand during cooking.

Decorate each biscuit with a sliver of almond and bake for 20-30 minutes. Allow to cool slightly, then carefully remove biscuits with their rice paper bases (which are edible) and cool them completely on a wire rack. Store in an airtight tin.

◄ Hazelnut and apricot crunch

Apricot Tart

INGREDIENTS *serves 4-6*
2½ cups/600ml/1pt yoghurt
  shortcrust pastry to line a pan
  approximately 19cm/7½in
1½ cups/400g/14oz canned apricots
⅜ cup/90ml/3½fl oz whipping cream
2 tbsp/30ml cornflour
¼ cup/50g/2oz castor sugar
1 tbsp/15ml lemon juice
2 tsp/10ml vanilla extract
1 egg, separated

METHOD
Drain the yoghurt for 3 hours. Bake the pastry case for 10 minutes. Drain the fruit (save the juice for use in a fruit salad) and lay the apricot halves on the pastry. When the yoghurt has drained, mix it together with the whipped cream and remaining ingredients except the egg white, beating everything to a smooth mixture.

Whisk the egg white until it is stiff and fold it into the other mixture. Spoon it over the apricots and bake at 325°F/170°C/Gas 3 for 50 minutes.

VARIATION
Use curd cheese or quark (1⅓ cups/225g/8oz) instead of the yoghurt if preferred.

▲ Apricot tart

Danish Apple Pie

INGREDIENTS *serves 4-6*
shortcrust pastry to line a pan
  approximately 19cm/7½in
5 medium/700g/1½lb cooking apples,
  peeled, cored and sliced
¼ cup/50ml/2oz water
¼ cup/50g/2oz sugar
1 tbsp/½oz butter
1 tsp/5ml ground cinnamon
1 cup/250ml/8fl oz soured cream
2 tbsp/30ml castor sugar

METHOD
Bake the pastry for 10 minutes at 350°F/180°C/Gas 4. Make a thick apple sauce using the apples, water, sugar, butter and half of the cinnamon. There shouldn't be any excess liquid when the apples are cooked, but if there is, cook for a few minutes more without a lid, stirring to prevent the apples sticking.

Let the apple sauce cool a little before turning into the pie shell. Spoon the soured cream over the apples. Mix the rest of the cinnamon with the sugar and sprinkle this over the soured cream. Bake at 400°F/200°C/Gas 6 for 30 minutes.

This is best served warm, rather than straight from the oven, but it is also good cold.

French Apple Tart

INGREDIENTS *serves 6*
¾ cup/75g/3oz plain untreated flour
¾ cup/75g/3oz wholewheat flour
⅓ cup/50g/2oz ground almonds
8 tbsp/100g/4oz butter, softened
1 egg
¼ cup/50g/2oz fruit sugar
pinch salt

THE FILLING
6 cooking apples
10 tbsp/150g/5oz butter
2-3 tbsp/30-45ml fruit sugar
2 tsp/10ml mixed spice

METHOD
Pre-heat the oven to 400°F/200°C/Gas 6. To make the pastry, sift the flours and almonds together onto a board and make a well in the middle. Put the remaining ingredients into the well and work in with your fingertips until you have a smooth dough. Knead for a few minutes, then leave for half an hour in the fridge.

Meanwhile, peel, core and slice the apples. Heat the butter in a pan and fry the apples gently until soft and golden.

Add the sugar and spice and cook, stirring, until the apple is coated with syrup.

Line a greased 8in/22cm loose-bottomed quiche pan with the pastry and fill with the apple. Bake for 25-30 minutes and serve with whipped cream.

Chocolate Cake

INGREDIENTS *serves 6*
1/2 cup/100g/4oz butter or soft margarine
3/4 cup/175g/6oz sugar
2 eggs, beaten
2 1/4 cups/225g/8oz flour
1 tsp/5ml baking powder
4 tbsp/50g/2oz cocoa
1 tsp/5ml bicarbonate of soda
1 cup/225ml/8fl oz yoghurt
1 tsp/5ml vanilla extract

METHOD
Beat the butter and sugar together until light. Add the eggs and continue beating. Sieve the flour, baking powder, cocoa and bicarbonate, and mix it into the butter mixture. Add the yoghurt and vanilla extract, mix in thoroughly.

Turn the mixture into a well greased cake pan, measuring approximately 8in/20cm. (Use two sandwich pans or a large ring mould if preferred.) Bake at 350°F/180°C/Gas 4 for 25 minutes. Insert a knife to test and cook a little longer if necessary. Timing obviously depends on the type of pan used.

Cool and ice with Cream Cheese Frosting or serve sprinkled with icing sugar.

Fruit Tartlets

INGREDIENTS *serves 6-8*
6-8 small pie shells, baked
2/3 cup/100g/4oz cream cheese
1/2 tsp/2.5ml vanilla extract (optional)
1-2 tsp/5-10ml castor sugar
3-4 cups/450g/1lb fresh fruit (raspberries, grapes, strawberries, redcurrants etc)
apricot jam to glaze

METHOD
Mix the cream cheese with the vanilla and just enough sugar to make a mixture the consistency of thick cream. Spoon into the baked and cooled pie shells. Cover the cream cheese with fresh fruit (de-pip the grapes). Melt a little apricot jam in a saucepan and brush over the fruit to glaze it.

Use a selection of different fruits to make an attractive plate of pastries. You could also make one large pie and fill the pie shell with alternate rings of different fruits.

Buttermilk Spice Cake

INGREDIENTS *serves 6*
2 1/4 cups/300g/10oz flour
1 cup/225g/8oz sugar
1 1/2 tsp/7.5ml bicarbonate of soda
1 tsp/5ml baking powder
pinch salt
1 tsp/5ml ground cinnamon
1/2 tsp/2.5ml ground cloves
1/2 cup/100g/4oz butter, melted
1 1/2 cups/350ml/12fl oz buttermilk
2 eggs

METHOD
Sift the dry ingredients together. Add the butter and buttermilk and beat the mixture until it is smooth. Pour the batter into a greased and floured cake pan measuring approximately 8in/20cm. Bake at 350°F/180°C/Gas 4 for 40 minutes.

Pumpkin, Sunflower and Raisin Cake

INGREDIENTS *serves 6-8*
2 1/4 cups/350g/12oz pumpkin
2 1/4 cups/225g/8oz wholewheat flour
pinch salt
2 tsp/10ml baking powder
1 tsp/5ml bicarbonate of soda
1/3 cup/50g/2oz sunflower seeds, chopped
1/3 cup/50g/2oz raisins
2 eggs
2 tbsp/30ml honey
2 tbsp/30ml molasses
1 tbsp/15ml warm water

METHOD
Pre-heat the oven to 375°F/190°C/Gas 5. Peel the pumpkin, cut into smallish pieces and boil until tender. Drain and cut up finely.

Combine flour, salt, baking powder, sunflower seeds and raisins and mix well.

In another bowl, beat the eggs and stir in the honey and molasses. Add 1 tbsp/15ml of warm water with the pumpkin and beat well.

Mix all the ingredients together thoroughly and pour into a greased and floured tin. Bake for 50-60 minutes until done. Allow to stand for 10 minutes in the tin, then cool on a wire rack.

Pecan Pie

INGREDIENTS *serves 4-6*
1 1/2 cups/250g/8oz pastry
4 tbsp/50g/1oz butter, softened
2 tbsp/30ml honey
2 tbsp/30ml maple syrup
3 eggs
1 tsp/5ml vanilla essence
1 cup/100g/4oz pecan halves
whipped cream

METHOD
Pre-heat the oven to 425°F/220°C/Gas 7. Line a 8 1/2 in/22cm tin with the chosen pastry. Prick and bake blind for 10 minutes.

Meanwhile, make the filling. Beat the butter together with the honey and syrup until smooth. In another bowl, beat the eggs and vanilla essence thoroughly with a wire or rotary whisk. Pour in the syrup, beating constantly with a fork.

Scatter the nuts evenly over the pastry base and pour the custard over. Bake in the middle of the oven for 10 minutes. Reduce the heat to 325°F/160°C/Gas 3 and bake for a further 25-35 minutes until the filling is set, but not dry. Serve warm (but not hot) or cold with whipped cream.

Yoghurt Cake

INGREDIENTS *serves 4*
5/8 cup/150ml/1/4pt yoghurt
2 1/2 cups/250g/9oz flour
3 tsp/15ml baking powder
1/4 cup/60ml/2 1/2fl oz oil
3/4 cup/175g/6oz sugar
1 tsp/5ml vanilla extract
2 eggs

METHOD
Mix everything together well. Beat until smooth. Turn the mixture into a well-greased cake pan measuring approximately 20cm/8in. Bake at 180°C/350°F/Gas 4 for 45 minutes. Insert a knife to test and cook a little longer if necessary.

This is a good basic recipe with many variations. To make an upside-down fruit cake sprinkle the bottom of the pan with brown sugar and lay sliced apples, pears or canned pineapple on the sugar, cover with the cake mixture and cook as directed.

Blackcurrant Froth

INGREDIENTS
²/₃ cup/150ml/¹/₄pt yoghurt
2 eggs, separated
1 tbsp/15ml crème de cassis (or
    blackcurrant syrup)
¹/₄ cup/50g/2oz castor sugar
2 cups/225g/8oz blackcurrants

METHOD
Stir the yoghurt and egg yolks together with
the crème de cassis and sugar until the sugar
is dissolved.

Just before serving, whisk the egg whites
until stiff and fold them into the yolk
mixture. Fold the blackcurrants in gently.
Spoon into individual dishes.

Serve with sponge fingers or cookies.

VARIATION
Change the flavours by using a different
liqueur: orange liqueur with a little grated
orange rind; chocolate liqueur with some
grated chocolate. If you want to prepare this
some time before serving it, refrigerate the
yolk mixture and add the whites and
currants at the last minute.

▲ Blackcurrant froth

Orange Chiffon

INGREDIENTS *serves 4-6*
1 tbsp/15ml agar-agar
¹/₂ cup/100ml/4fl oz orange juice
5 tbsp/75ml castor sugar
2 eggs, separated
1 cup/250ml/8fl oz buttermilk
grated orange peel

METHOD
Soak the agar-agar in orange juice. Heat
this gently until the agar-agar is dissolved.
Remove the pan from the heat. Beat 3 tbsp/
45ml sugar with the yolks until light and
fluffy. Add this to the agar-agar mixture and
stir it over a very low heat until it begins to
thicken. Pour the thickened mixture into a
bowl and add the buttermilk and orange
peel. Mix together and chill until it is
beginning to set.

Beat the egg whites until they are stiff.
Fold in the remaining sugar. Combine the
egg whites and the agar-agar mixture,
stirring gently.

Turn the chiffon into a serving dish (or use
individual glasses) and refrigerate until
required.

VARIATION
If you prefer you can make a pie by turning
this mixture into a baked pie crust and
refrigerating it in the crust. Decorate the
chiffon with slivers of candied fruit or
chocolate.

Orange Cream

INGREDIENTS *serves 4*
2 eggs, separated
2 tbsp/30ml castor sugar
juice and grated rind of 1 orange
1¹/₃ cups/225g/8oz cream cheese
2 tbsp/30ml orange-flavoured liqueur

METHOD
Beat the yolks with the sugar until they are
thick and creamy. Add the orange juice and
rind and mix it in well. Soften the cheese and
add it to the egg mixture. Add the liqueur.

Beat the whites until they are stiff. Fold in
a little of the beaten whites to the cheese
mixture and then gently fold in the rest.
Spoon into four glasses and serve

immediately.

If you want to prepare this in advance,
leave the egg whites until just before you are
going to serve, and whisk the whites and
fold them into the cheese mixture at the very
last minute. If you make it in advance with
the egg whites it may separate - if this
happens, stir through before serving.

VARIATION
Use curd cheese or quark for a less rich
version.

Rhubarb Cream Jelly

INGREDIENTS *serves 6*
2¹/₂ cups/600ml/1pt yoghurt
4 cups/450g/1lb rhubarb
sugar to taste
1 tsp/5ml vanilla essence
¹/₂ tsp/2.5ml ground cinnamon or a
    small piece of cinnamon stick
1 cup/250ml/8fl oz whipping cream,
    whipped
2 tbsp/15g/¹/₂oz agar-agar
2 tbsp/30ml boiling water

METHOD
Drain the yoghurt for about 3 hours.

Cook the rhubarb with the sugar, vanilla
essence and cinnamon with just enough
water to stop it from burning. You will need
1¹/₄ cups/300ml/¹/₂pt of cooked rhubarb.
Mix the cooked rhubarb with the drained
yoghurt and the whipped cream. Mix
gently until everything is combined.

Dissolve the agar-agar in the boiling
water, mixing well until smooth. Add to the
rhubarb mixture, stirring the agar-agar in
quickly.

Turn the mixture into a moistened small
ring mould and chill until set. Serve with
more whipped cream if desired.

VARIATION
Use 1¹/₃ cups/225g/8oz quark, fromage
blanc or curd cheese if preferred instead of
the drained yoghurt.

Crème Caramel

INGREDIENTS *serves 6*
4 tbsp/60ml fruit sugar
4 tbsp/60ml water

THE CUSTARD
600ml/20fl oz milk
few drops vanilla essence
4 eggs
3 tbsp/45ml fruit sugar

METHOD
Pre-heat the oven to 350°F/180°C/Gas 4. For the caramel, put the sugar and the water in a heavy saucepan and stir over a low heat until the sugar has dissolved. Bring to the boil and boil until the syrup is golden. Pour the caramel into six individual moulds (or one large one) and swirl it around so that it coats the bottom and sides.

Bring the milk and vanilla essence to the boil in a saucepan. Remove from the heat.

Beat the eggs and sugar together in a bowl. Gradually add the hot milk, stirring all the while.

Strain or ladle the custard into the moulds. Stand them in a roasting tin half filled with hot water and bake for 45 minutes until set. Allow to cool and then chill. Don't turn out the crème caramel until you are ready to serve or it will lose its gloss.

▼ Crème caramel

Rose Petal Trifle

INGREDIENTS *serves 6*
2 eggs
4 tbsp/50g/2oz dark brown muscovado
   sugar
½ tsp/2.5ml ground cinnamon
4 tbsp/25g/1oz wholemeal flour
4 tbsp/25g/1oz plain flour
1 tbsp/15g/½oz polyunsaturated
   margarine, melted
2 egg yolks
2 tbsp/15g/½oz cornflour
2 tbsp/25g/1oz light muscovado sugar
1¼ cups/300ml/½pt skimmed milk
1 tbsp/15ml triple strength rose water
4 passion fruit, halved
6oz/175g raspberries
2 tbsp/30ml whipping cream, whipped
   or strained Greek yoghurt
rose petals

METHOD

Line and lightly grease an 18cm/7in sandwich tin. Whisk the eggs and dark muscovado sugar together, until thick and creamy.

Fold in the cinnamon, flours and melted margarine. Pour into the tin and bake in a pre-heated oven at 350°F/180°C/Gas 4 for 20 minutes, or until risen and firm. Turn out and cool.

Beat the egg yolks, cornflour and light muscovado sugar together. Heat the milk until boiling and pour on to the egg mix. Return to the saucepan and cook, stirring continuously, over a gentle heat until thickened.

Add the rose water, cover and set aside until cold.

Cut the sponge into cubes and place in the base of a serving dish. Scoop the flesh from the passion fruit and spoon over the sponge. Top with raspberries.

Pour over the custard and pipe the cream, or spoon the yoghurt on top. Garnish with rose petals and serve.

Raspberry and Apple Layer

INGREDIENTS *serves 6*
1lb/450g dessert apples, peeled, cored
   and chopped
8oz/225g ripe raspberries, puréed
1 tbsp/15ml light muscovado sugar
2 tbsp/25g/1oz polyunsaturated
   margarine
2oz/50g wholemeal breadcrumbs
4oz/100g muesli biscuits, crushed
1 tsp/5ml mixed spice
raspberries
green apple slices

METHOD

Place the apples in a saucepan with 1 tbsp/15ml water, cover and gently cook until tender. Beat or process in a liquidizer or food processor to a purée.

Mix with the raspberry purée and sugar. Leave to cool.

Melt the margarine in a saucepan, add the breadcrumbs and stir over a low heat until browned. Stir in the muesli biscuits and mixed spice. Place the fruit purée and crumb mix in alternate layers in glass bowls. Decorate with fruit and serve.

Banana and Cherry Yoghurt

INGREDIENTS *serves 4*
4 very ripe bananas, cut into pieces
2 tsp/10ml lemon juice
1¼ cups/300ml/½pt natural low fat
   yoghurt
8oz/225g fresh cherries, pitted
cherry pairs with stalks

METHOD

Mash the bananas with the lemon juice. Mix in the yoghurt.

Divide the pitted cherries between four tall glasses and top with the banana yoghurt.

Hang a pair of cherries over the edge of each glass to decorate. Serve chilled, alone or with wholemeal biscuits.

Berry Meringue

INGREDIENTS *serves 4-6*
crushed meringues to line a 7in/18cm
   baking dish
2½ cups/350g/12oz blackberries
⅔ cup/150ml/¼pt soured cream
2 tsp/10ml castor sugar
½ tsp/2.5ml vanilla essence

METHOD

Line the baking dish with the crushed meringues. Cover with the blackberries. Mix the soured cream, sugar and vanilla essence together and spoon this over the berries. Bake at 350°F/180°C/Gas 4 for 20 minutes.

NOTE

If you are a frequent baker of meringues you may well suffer from a surfeit of crushed meringues - here is the answer to the problem. Other berries would do but blackberries have the particular acidity which contrasts with the sweetness of the meringues.

▲▲ Banana and cherry yoghurt
▲ Raspberry and apple layer

Noodle Pudding

INGREDIENTS *serves 6*
1 cup/175g/6oz cottage cheese
½ cup/75g/3oz cream cheese
⅔ cup/150ml/¼pt soured cream
3 eggs
½ cup/100g/4oz sugar
3½ cups/350g/12oz flat noodles, cooked
    and drained
½ cup/75g/3oz raisins or sultanas
4 tbsp/50g/2oz butter or margarine,
    melted
1 tsp/5ml ground cinnamon
1 tsp/5ml sugar

METHOD
Mix the cottage and cream cheese with the
soured cream. Beat the eggs and sugar
together and add them to the cheese
mixture. Fold in the cooked noodles and
raisins.

Turn the mixture into a buttered
ovenproof dish. Pour on the melted butter.
Mix the cinnamon and sugar together and
sprinkle it over the top of the noodle
mixture. Bake at 350°F/180°C/Gas 4 for 1
hour. Serve hot.

VARIATION
This hearty Central European pudding has
many variations. Add chopped apples or
soaked dried apricots to the mixture before
baking. Vary the cheese mixture to include
more cottage cheese or use curd cheese
instead of the cream cheese.

Brown Rice Pudding

INGREDIENTS *serves 4*
½ cup/100g/4oz brown rice
2½ cups/600ml/1pt China tea
1 stick cinnamon
⅓ cup/50g/2oz sultanas
⅜ cup/50g/2oz dried apricots, chopped
¼ cup/50g/2oz almonds
sliced fresh fruit (optional)

METHOD
Wash the rice thoroughly under running
water. Put it in a heavy pan with the tea and
simmer gently for about an hour with the
cinnamon.

Pre-heat the oven to 350°F/180°C/Gas 4.
Remove the cinnamon and transfer the rice
to an ovenproof dish. Stir in the remaining
ingredients and bake for about 25 minutes
until done. Serve hot or refrigerate and serve
cold. Garnish with sliced fresh fruit, if liked.

Apple Pudding

INGREDIENTS *serves 4-6*
2½ cups/600ml/1pt yoghurt
⅔ cup/150ml/¼pt whipping cream
2 eggs
4 tbsp/75g/3oz castor sugar
grated lemon rind
1 large cooking apple, peeled and sliced
½ tsp/2.5ml ground cinnamon
2 tbsp/25g/1oz sugar

METHOD
Drain the yoghurt for about 4 hours. Whip
the cream and fold it into the drained
yoghurt. Beat the eggs with the sugar and
lemon rind and add to the yoghurt mixture.

Turn into a greased shallow oven dish.
Lay the apple slices on top of the yoghurt
mixture. Scatter cinnamon on top and then
the sugar.

Bake at 350°F/180°C/Gas 4 for 50
minutes. Serve warm.

▶ Baked apple